CRYSTAL
PRESCRIPTIONS

The A–Z guide to
over 1,200 symptoms and
their healing crystals

JUDY HALL

EW
QUALITY NATURALLY

O
BOOKS

WINCHESTER UK
NEW YORK USA

JOHN HUNT PUBLISHING

First published by O-Books, 2006
O-Books is an imprint of John Hunt Publishing Ltd., No. 3 East St., Alresford,
Hampshire SO24 9EE, UK
office@jhpbooks.com
www.johnhuntpublishing.com
www.o-books.com

For distributor details and how to order please visit the 'Ordering' section on our
website.

ISBN: 978 1 90504 740 6
978 1 84694 629 5 (ebook)

A CIP catalogue record for this book is available from the British Library.

Design: BookDesign™, London

UK: Printed and bound by CPI Group (UK) Ltd, Croydon, CR0 4YY
US: Printed and bound by Thomson-Shore, 7300 West Joy Road, Dexter, MI 48130

We operate a distinctive and ethical publishing philosophy
in all areas of our business, from our global network of
authors to production and worldwide distribution.

DISCLAIMER

The information given in this directory is in no
way intended to be a substitute for treatment by a
medical practitioner. Further assistance should be
sought from a suitably qualified crystal healer.

CONTENTS

Volumes in this series:

Crystal Prescriptions
The A–Z guide to over 1,200 symptoms and their healing crystals
ISBN: 978-1-90504-740-6 (Paperback) £7.99 $15.95

Crystal Prescriptions volume 2
The A–Z guide to over 1,250 conditions and their new
generation healing crystals
ISBN: 978-1-78279-560-5 (Paperback) £8.99 $14.95

Crystal Prescriptions volume 3
Crystal solutions to electromagnetic pollution and geopathic stress.
An A–Z guide.
ISBN: 978-1-78279-791-3 (Paperback) £8.99 $14.95

Crystal Prescriptions volume 4
The A–Z guide to the chakra balancing crystals and kundalini
activation stones
ISBN: 978-1-78535-053-5 (Paperback) £10.99 $17.95

Crystal Prescriptions volume 5
Space clearing, Feng Shui and Psychic Protection.
An A-Z guide.
ISBN: 978-1-78535-457-1 (Paperback) £12.99 $19.95

Crystal Prescriptions volume 6
Crystals for ancestral clearing, soul retrieval, spirit release and karmic
healing. An A-Z guide.
ISBN: 978-1-78535-455-7 (Paperback) £13.99 $19.95

Crystal Prescriptions volume 7
The A-Z Guide to Creating Crystal Essences for Abundant
Well-Being, Environmental Healing and Astral Magic
ISBN: 978-1-78904-052-4 (Paperback) £17.99 $29.95

PART I

CRYSTAL KNOW-HOW

Are you looking for gentle, non-invasive remedies for everyday ailments? Do you want first aid that works quickly and has no side effects? Have you ever had a headache and wondered how to ease it without drugs? Have you suffered from a virus for which there was no medical prescription? Have you felt depressed and out of sorts but did not want to resort to addictive pills? Have you suffered from stress? Does your child need a pacifier that is wholesome and safe? Have you suffered from anger and needed to dissipate it harmlessly? Have you discovered that past-life dis-ease is affecting your present health? Does your soul need uplifting, your chakras balancing? Are you looking for healthy attitudes and positive emotions?

Crystals are the answer, but the difficulty up until now has been in matching the remedy to the symptom you are experiencing.

Not any longer!

Whether you are a newcomer to the crystal world or an experienced healer, this directory will help you to find exactly what you need – a much easier process than may appear at first sight, and you only need a small number of crystals to heal most common conditions.

WHAT DOES THIS DIRECTORY DO?

The directory matches your condition to the crystal that can heal it, whether the problem is physical, emotional, mental or spiritual. It is a first-aid guide rather than a course in crystal healing, and it is based on sound principles that have been practised for millennia. While crystal healing does not deal primarily with specific conditions, being an holistic-based system, crystals can ameliorate symptoms – and will also deal with the disturbance on more subtle levels, often bringing to light the underlying causes of the condition.

In the pages that follow you will find symptoms listed alphabetically together with appropriate crystals to ease your malady, whether it is of the body, emotions, mind or soul. Crystals are also included that will bring about a positive improvement in energy, attitudes, emotions, and so on.

WHY ARE SO MANY CRYSTALS INCLUDED?

In some instances, several crystals are listed to heal conditions in this directory. This is because all possibilities have been included to give you the widest choice, and to utilize crystals you may already have. It also gives you an opportunity to choose crystals that suit your budget and your lifestyle.

IS IT EXPENSIVE?

Some crystals are more readily available, and much cheaper, than others (and see Crystals for Health page 14). Certain crystals can be expensive, especially the rarer or higher-vibration stones, but you can use alternatives. It is not necessary to buy gem-quality stones, for instance. Tumbled opaque Emerald or Ruby can be as effective as a faceted gem and costs a fraction of the price. The section on Finding Your Prescription (page 20) tells you how to select exactly the right stone for your purpose, whether at a crystal store or from your own collection. Instructions are given on pages 49–52 for making crystal remedies, an easily assimilated form of crystal energy; and on pages 43–48 for placing your crystals to bring about optimum health.

WHERE SHOULD I OBTAIN MY CRYSTALS?

Crystals are readily available from stores or via the internet. When choosing your crystal, remember that looks aren't everything. A misshapen lump can be as effective, or more so, as a beautiful stone. If you do obtain crystals via the web, be sure to choose a reputable supplier – you will find suggestions at the back of this book – and to check the size carefully. The advantage of buying crystals from a store is that you can select the one that feels right to you.

HOW DO I KNOW WHICH CRYSTAL IS RIGHT FOR ME?

Certain crystals have been underlined – these are particularly recommended for that specific condition or for general healing of the organ in question, and pendulum dowsing or finger dowsing is a simple way of pinpointing the right crystal for yourself or other people (see pages 24–26). See page 54 for examples of finding and using the right crystal.

DO I HAVE TO USE A PARTICULAR TYPE OF CRYSTAL?

You can use rough cut, tumbled or faceted stones as all have equal healing energy, although the clearer and purer the crystal energy is, the better will be the result. This is not in any way related to how a crystal *looks* on the surface. It is about how it *feels* and the power it radiates, and you will soon learn to recognize a powerful healing stone from the way it tingles when you touch it or the heat it generates in your hand. Tumbled stones feel nicer than rough cut when placed on your skin, while faceted are best set in silver or gold to wear for long periods; however, some stones need to touch the skin (see page 48). Remember to focus the energy of your crystal prior to use and to purify it afterwards (see pages 28–35).

A clear Quartz that has an unchipped point, together with a stone selected from each of the red, yellow, orange, green, blue and brown range of crystals, makes an excellent and inexpensive crystal healing first-aid kit.

DO ALL CRYSTALS HAVE THE SAME EFFECT?

Not every crystal will have the same effect on everyone who uses it. Certain stones have a finer vibration than others, particularly the more recent discoveries such as Petalite or Shattuckite. These finer-vibration stones tend to work on the subtle bodies that surround the physical body, but physical bodies themselves have different kinds of vibrations. If someone has regularly practised yoga, tai chi, healing or meditation, for instance, their vibrations will be more ethereal than someone who has done no spiritual work at all; and habitual attitudes and emotions profoundly affect the physical body. So, different crystal vibes suit different body types. The easiest way to find exactly the right stone for you is to dowse, either with a pendulum or by finger dowsing.

DO CRYSTALS NEED SPECIAL TREATMENT?

The power of crystals can be greatly enhanced by treating them with respect and recognizing that they are powerful beings – and by focusing their energies to the highest good of all concerned. You will find precise instructions for attuning your crystals to your unique vibration on page 33, but this can be adapted to anyone else who is going to use the crystal. If another person holds or works with your crystals, it is vital that you purify them after use and re-attune them to your own energy once again. It is also sensible to purify stones each time you use them yourself (see page 29).

CRYSTALS FOR HEALTH

Crystals have an important role in preventing disease and keeping you healthy, but if you do succumb to illness, they are a gentle but effective healing tool. Healing can be defined as bringing the body, emotions, mind and spirit back into harmony. It does not necessarily imply a cure, although it frequently ameliorates conditions. Crystal healing is a gentle and non-invasive process that creates balance on all levels, and one that can provide support to the body's own internal healing systems. The lore on which it is based has its roots in antiquity and the body of knowledge is, therefore, supported by thousands of years of practical experience.

Crystals interact with the human energy field to heal, calm, stimulate or adjust the energies within it and to bring the body back into balance. They are beneficial for children, animals, adults and the environment. Crystals also work on attitudes, emotions and the mind, instilling a feeling of well-being, neutralizing negativity, lifting depression and assisting coordination – both mental and physical. One of their most important roles in healing is in bringing the chakras and subtle energy sheath around the physical body back into alignment, and another is in dealing with underlying factors in dis-ease – the psychosomatic effect of the mind and emotions on the body.

Exactly how they do this is still something of a mystery, despite their having been used for this purpose for thousands of years, but the major explanations centre around three things: vibration, colour and mineral constituents.

VIBRATION

Each crystal has its own unique vibration, which can be felt by sensitive people, and most have a small but measurable electrical charge together with an internal lattice-like structure that absorbs and transforms toxic energies.

Virtually all crystals were born deep in the earth, inside the earth's magnetic field, so it's not surprising that they absorbed its magnetic charge and stellar radiation. However, the unique way in which each type of crystal developed subtly altered its magnetic charge. Some were produced, or amended, by great heat or pressure; others were laid down gradually over aeons of time; one or two arrived from outer space. Each cell within the human body also has an electrical charge and when the charge of a crystal is brought close to a cell, or to the biomagnetic sheath that surrounds the physical body, it gently brings the energy of the cell or the biomagnetic sheath back into balance.

MINERAL CONSTITUENTS

Crystals are formed from specific minerals, or combinations of minerals, and the chemical constitution of the stones, and their healing effect, was recognized in ancient Egypt and underlies crystal healing lore. Peridot, for instance, known as poor-man's Emerald because it shares its more expensive counterpart's brilliant green colour, is formed from silicon, iron and magnesium; while Tourmaline contains iron, boron, aluminium, lithium, magnesium, potassium, silicon, sodium and trace elements that affect the colour; and Turquoise is mainly aluminium with copper and iron. These minerals, which are essential for body health and physiological processes, pass into the body in minute dilutions (see Crystals for Health, page 14) and subtly affect health.

Kunzite, with its high lithium content, mimics the taking of a conventional lithium prescription in homoeopathic dosage to control the mood swings of bi-polar disorder.

It is important that stones with significant mineral content are placed, or worn, touching the skin rather than outside clothing (see list on page 48).

COLOUR

For thousands of years, energy centres, known as the chakras, have been identified on the human body and it has long been recognized that if a chakra is out of balance, it will cause dis-ease of a physical, emotional, mental or spiritual nature according to the chakra concerned. Each chakra resonates to a different colour – the base to red, the sacral to orange, the solar plexus to yellow and so on (see Chakras, pages 36–42), and when the appropriate colour crystal is placed on the chakra, it brings it back into balance and alignment.

In addition, the colour of the stone also plays a part in its healing effect. Deep-purple Amethyst, for instance, bears a resemblance to wine, and the stone has been renowned since ancient times for its sobering effect, counteracting the effects of over-indulgence and lifting the spirits. Red stones both energize and, paradoxically, calm, drawing off anger and discord. Blood-coloured, they were traditionally associated with haemorrhage and inflammation. Blue was seen as the colour of heaven, having a tonic effect, and counteracting the effect of the spirits of darkness. Yellow stones were associated with bilious disorders, jaundice and the liver; while soothing green was seen to have a powerful effect on tired and disordered eyes.

ASTROLOGICAL CORRESPONDENCES

Some crystals have astrological correspondences that also go back thousands of years. The crystal is aligned to a planet, or to a zodiac sign, that 'rules' the part of the body concerned and that is, therefore, beneficial to its proper functioning as it draws the celestial energy into the physical plane. In the East, gemstones are still used to correct imbalances that are identified from the natal chart. While you do not need to concern yourself with these correspondences, you can benefit from the astrological knowledge that has been incorporated into this directory.

LIKE CURES LIKE

In herbal medicine, herbs are used that correspond to the 'doctrine of signatures'. That is, the herbs look like organs of the body or bear a resemblance to a condition. In homoeopathy, minute doses are given of a substance that would cause the symptoms they are treating if used in quantity. Similarly, some crystals heal through appearance or through homoeopathic resonance. One particular form of Magnesite, for instance, looks exactly like a brain and is excellent for migraines and epilepsy, and Dendritic Agate, with its branching 'foliage', supports the nerves and blood vessels and is particularly useful in conditions like capillary degeneration.

Other crystals heal because their mineral content passes into the body as a trace element similar to that already in the body, or as a homoeopathic resonance. Malachite can assist arthritis as it passes minute dilutions of copper into the body. However, Malachite is a toxic stone, which is why a polished stone should be used, most of the treatment taking place at a vibrational level only.

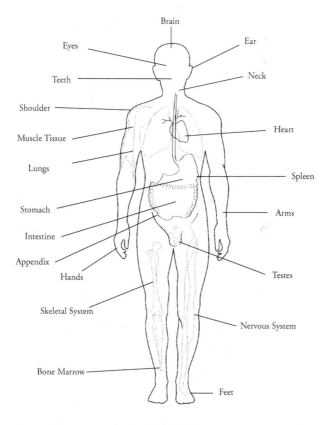

Anatomy Diagram

FINDING YOUR PRESCRIPTION

Many of the entries in this directory offer a choice of crystals to assist a particular condition. While all the stones listed could potentially help you, selecting exactly the right crystal is crucial if you are to obtain maximum benefit and the fastest relief. Some crystals have a much finer vibration than others and some work at a physical level while others operate more subtly – frequently bringing underlying causes to the surface that may mean you need to use a series of crystals.

You may find that you are instinctively drawn to a particular stone and it may be one that you already have in your collection. If so, try this one first. If it does not work as well as you would like, you can dowse for a suitable stone. You can also dowse when purchasing a healing crystal, either by allowing your fingers instinctively to pick the right stone from a number of stones – usually the one that 'sticks' to them – or using a pendulum or finger dowsing. Dowsing is an excellent way to select your crystal(s) and you can either use a pendulum for this purpose or finger dowse. Both methods use the ability of your intuitive body–mind connection to tune into subtle vibrations and to influence your hands. A focused mind, trust in the process, carefully worded questions and a clear intent will support your dowsing and your healing.

USING YOUR CRYSTALS FOR HEALING

Most crystals can be placed over clothing and left in place for 20 minutes or so (see pages 43-48 for healing placements and page 27 for how to dowse for the appropriate length of time to leave a stone in place), although many are particularly beneficial when placed directly on skin. They can also be taped in place, or worn for much longer periods for healing or prevention; or they can be kept in a pocket, or placed around your bed or a room. You can also apply crystal remedies externally, or take them internally. These remedies convey crystal vibes to the body at a subtle level and are particularly effective for emotional conditions. If your crystal has a point, place it point towards yourself, or point down if placed on your body, to draw healing or re-energizing properties into your body; and point out, or up if placed on your body, to draw off toxic residues or emotions.

DOWSING

FRAMING YOUR QUESTION

Framing your question appropriately is essential if you are to select exactly the right crystal for your purpose and achieve the most beneficial result. Your questions need to be precise and unambiguous and be capable of a straight 'yes' or 'no' answer. They also need to be asked with serious intent. An irresponsible approach or a frivolous question is unlikely to reveal anything of lasting benefit and could actually do harm as crystals are powerful tools. They should be treated with respect.

Take time to prepare yourself to ask the question. Sit quietly for a few moments, bringing your focus away from the outside world and quietening your mind. Word your question precisely and carefully.

If you are not specific enough in your questioning and, for instance, ask: 'Is this the right crystal for me?', the answer could well be 'yes' but it may not refer to the ailment you wish to relieve at that moment. It could indicate a crystal that would give you long-term benefit for an, as yet, unrecognized condition that exists at the physical, emotional, mental or soul level. That crystal could well be of value to you, but it would not heal the immediate symptom.

You need to be specific. If you are finger dowsing ask: 'Is

[name of crystal] the best and most appropriate crystal to treat my headache at this moment?' If you are pendulum dowsing, ask: 'Please show me the best and most appropriate crystal to treat my headache now.' It can also be worthwhile enquiring: 'Is there a deeper condition underlying my symptom?' If the answer is 'yes', you can ask: 'Does this condition lie at the physical [wait for a moment for the pendulum to respond], emotional [wait for a moment], mental [wait for a moment] or soul [wait for a moment] level?' You can then put your finger on each letter in the directory in turn. When you find a 'yes' response, run your finger down the page until the pendulum locates the underlying cause of your dis-ease.

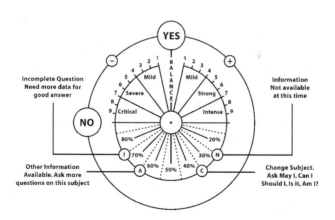

Dowsing the list

where a pendulum might provoke unwanted attention. This method of dowsing works particularly well for people who are kinaesthetic, that is to say their body responds intuitively to subtle feelings, but anyone can learn to finger dowse.

To finger dowse

To finger dowse, hold the thumb and first finger of your right hand together (see illustration). Loop the thumb and finger of your left hand through to make a 'chain'. Ask your question clearly and unambiguously – you can speak it aloud or keep it within your mind. Now pull gently but firmly. If the chain breaks, the answer is 'no'. If it holds, the answer is 'yes'.

Finger dowsing

PENDULUM DOWSING

If you are familiar with pendulum dowsing, use the pendulum in your usual way. If you are not, this skill is easily learned.

To pendulum dowse

To pendulum dowse, hold your pendulum between the thumb and forefinger of your most receptive hand (in many people this is the left) with about a hand's length of chain hanging down to the pendulum (see illustration) – you will soon know what is the right length for you. Wrap the remaining chain around your fingers so that it does not obstruct the dowsing.

You will need to ascertain which is a 'yes' and which a 'no' response. Some people find that the pendulum swings in one direction for 'yes' and at right angles to that axis for 'no', while others have a backwards and forwards swing for one reply, and a circular motion for the other. A 'wobble' of the pendulum can indicate a 'maybe' or that it is not appropriate to dowse at that time, or that the wrong question is being asked (if the pendulum stops completely it is usually inappropriate to ask at that time). In which case, ask if it is appropriate, and if the answer is 'yes', check that you are framing the question in the correct way.

You can ascertain your particular pendulum response by holding the pendulum over your knee and asking: 'Is my name [correct name]?' The direction that the pendulum swings will indicate 'yes'. Check by asking: 'Is my name [incorrect name]?'

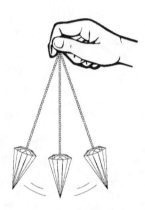

Holding the Pendulum, Establishing 'Yes' and 'No'

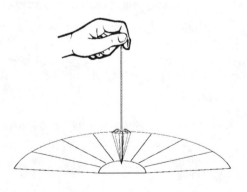

Dowsing over an Arc

To ascertain which crystal will be most beneficial for you, hold the pendulum in your most receptive hand and slowly run the forefinger of your other hand along the list of possible crystals, noting whether you get a 'yes' or 'no' response. Check the whole list to see which 'yes' response is strongest as there may well be several that would be appropriate and you may need to use several crystals in combination. Another way to do this, if you have several of the crystals available, is to touch each crystal in turn, again noting the 'yes' or 'no' response.

A pendulum can also be used to establish for how long a crystal should be left in place. This is particularly useful if you are placing the crystal over an organ or around your body, but it can also be helpful if you are wearing a crystal and need to know whether or not to wear it at night – in which case you will get a 'yes' or 'no' answer to the question: 'Should I remove this crystal at night?' To establish timing, use an arc on which you have marked five-minute or one-hour or one-day intervals (ask in advance whether the period should be checked in minutes, hours or days). Hold the hand with the pendulum over the centre of the arc and ask that the pendulum will go towards the correct period (see illustration).

PURIFYING AND
FOCUSING CRYSTALS

Crystals hold the energetic charge of everyone who comes into contact with them and they absorb emanations from their surroundings so, particularly when being used for healing, they need regular purifying. Although certain crystals, such as Quartz and Carnelian, are self-cleansing, it is sensible to purify and re-energize a crystal every time it is used. The method employed will depend on the type of crystal. Soft and friable crystals, for instance, and those that are attached to a base can be damaged by water and are best purified by a 'dry' process such as brown rice or sunlight, but many crystals benefit from being placed under running water or in the sea.

Crystals work best when their energy is harnessed and focused with intent towards the task at hand. By taking the time to attune a crystal to your own unique frequency, you enhance its vibratory effect and amplify its healing power.

Crystal being purified on a large Quartz cluster]

PURIFYING YOUR CRYSTAL

As crystals absorb energy and negative vibes, they need purifying after use as a healing tool, but crystals can also benefit from purifying before they are used to make sure they are giving an optimum performance. Always purify and focus a new crystal before use. Choose a method that is suitable for the type of crystal – layered or soft crystals, or those with many small points, for instance, should not be placed under running water and soft stones like Selenite will dissolve.

Running water

Hold your crystals under a running tap, or pour bottled water over them, or place in a stream or the ocean to draw off negative energy. You can also immerse appropriate crystals in the ocean or in a bowl of water into which a handful of sea salt or rock salt has been added. Dry the crystal carefully afterwards and place in the sun to re-energize.

Rice or salt

Place your crystal in a bowl of salt or brown rice and leave overnight for the negative energies to be absorbed. (Brush salt off carefully and make sure that it has been removed from any niches or cracks in the crystal as otherwise it will absorb water in the future and could cause splintering. Salt is best avoided if the crystal is layered or friable.) Place the crystals in the sun to re-energize.

Smudging

Sage, sweetgrass or joss sticks are excellent for smudging as they quickly remove negative energies. Light the smudge stick and pass it over the crystal if it is large, or hold the crystal in your hand in the smoke if it is small. It is traditional to fan the smoke gently with a feather but this is not essential.

Visualizing light

Hold your crystal in your hands and visualize a column of bright white light coming down and covering the crystal, absorbing anything negative it may have picked up and restoring the pure energy once more. If you find visualization difficult, you can use the light of a candle.

Crystal clearing remedies

A number of crystal clearing remedies are available from flower essence suppliers, crystal shops and the internet. The most effective of these is *Crystal Clear*, available from Petaltone Essences (see page 171). You can either drop the remedy directly onto the crystal, gently rubbing it over the crystal with your finger, or put a few drops into clean spring water in an atomiser or spray bottle and gently mist the crystal.

Purifyig Crystals

RE-ENERGIZING YOUR CRYSTAL

Crystals can be placed on Quartz or Carnelian to re-energize them but an excellent energizer is the light of the sun. Red and yellow crystals particularly enjoy being placed in the sun to energize them, and white and pale-coloured crystals respond well to the moon, but all crystals can benefit from a day of sunlight and white crystals can be left overnight in the light of the moon. (Be careful if you are placing crystals on a window sill to energize them. Sunlight focused through a crystal can be a fire hazard and delicate crystals will lose their colour quickly.) Some brown crystals such as Smoky Quartz, which are particularly well grounded, respond to being placed on or in the earth for a short time. If you bury a crystal, remember to mark its position clearly.

Enerfizing Crystals by the Light of the Sun

FOCUSING YOUR CRYSTAL

Once your crystal has been purified and re-energized, sit quietly holding the crystal in your hands for a few minutes until you feel in tune with it. Picture it surrounded by light and love. State that the crystal is dedicated to the highest good of all who use it. Then state very clearly your intention for the crystal – that it will heal or protect you, for instance. If it is intended for a specific purpose such as healing a particular symptom, state that also. Repeat the intention several times to anchor it into the crystal.

Focusing your Crystal

STORING YOUR CRYSTALS

A few crystals, such as Obsidian or Agate, can take rough handling, especially if they have been tumbled, but even these stones can become scratched or chipped and crystals respond best to being treated gently – particularly those that have points, facets or a multitude of tiny crystals or layers that can easily break off. While one or two tiny chips might not affect the energy of a crystal point, this particular shape focuses energy into a powerful beam and a chip could easily distort this beam, especially if the tip is damaged. Purpose-made crystal wands, which mimic a point, should also be kept free from chips or scratches.

Wrapping your crystals ensures that they will not pick up negative energy from the atmosphere or bad vibes from other people. Most crystals are best wrapped individually in tissue or a soft cloth and placed into a box for safe keeping, but tumbled stones can be kept together in a bag when not in use. If you add a Carnelian to the bag, your stones will always be purified, energized and ready to go to work.

Wrapping Crystals Individually

Keeping Crystals in a Bag

CRYSTALS AND THE CHAKRAS

The chakras are linkage points between your aura (the subtle bodies that form the biomagnetic sheath around your physical body) and your physical body. Mediating energy, each chakra links to a specific area of life and to various organs and conditions. The chakras below the waist are primarily physical, those in the upper torso are aligned to emotional functioning that can create psychosomatic conditions, and those in the head function on a mental and intuitive basis, although the third eye, slightly above and between the eyebrows, and the crown chakras also function at a spiritual level. Any imbalance, blockage or disturbance in these chakras creates dis-ease that will ultimately manifest in your physical body but which can be restored to equilibrium before physical illness results.

Traditionally, each chakra has its own colour, as shown on the illustration. By placing crystals of the appropriate colour and vibration on the chakras, chakra imbalances are quickly eliminated and the chakras are harmonized to work together, leading to better health and a sense of well-being.

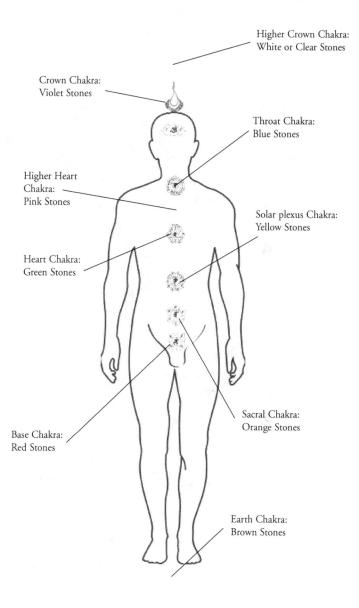

Higher Crown Chakra:
White or Clear Stones

Crown Chakra:
Violet Stones

Throat Chakra:
Blue Stones

Higher Heart
Chakra:
Pink Stones

Solar plexus Chakra:
Yellow Stones

Heart Chakra:
Green Stones

Sacral Chakra:
Orange Stones

Base Chakra:
Red Stones

Earth Chakra:
Brown Stones

Crystals and the Chakras

CHAKRA CONNECTIONS

Each chakra is connected to a specific area of life, and blockages or imbalances in a chakra create specific areas of dis-ease that can be healed by placing the appropriate colour crystal onto the chakra. If a chakra is stuck open it is known as a blown chakra and will lead to negative conditions as shown under each chakra. A blown chakra is particularly vulnerable to outside influence as there is no protection. Similarly, a chakra can be stuck in the closed position leading to blockages and negative qualities manifesting.

Earth chakra (beneath the feet)

The sphere of everyday reality and groundedness. Imbalances or blockages lead to discomfort in your physical body, feelings of helplessness, and inability to function practically in the world. Earth chakra imbalances pick up adverse environmental factors such as geopathic stress, 'black' ley lines and toxic pollutants.

Negative quality: powerlessness. *Positive quality:* empowerment.

Base chakra (base of your spine/perineum)

The sphere of basic survival instincts and security issues. Imbalances lead to sexual disturbances and feelings of anger, impotence and frustration.

Negative quality: insecurity. *Positive quality:* inner security.

Sacral chakra (navel) (slightly below your waist)

The sphere of creativity, fertility and acceptance of yourself as a sexual being. Imbalances lead to infertility and blocked creativity. The sacral chakra is where 'hooks' from other people may make themselves felt, particularly from sexual encounters.

Negative quality: low self-esteem. *Positive quality:* self-worth.

Solar plexus chakra (slightly above your waist)

The sphere of emotional communication and assimilation. Blockages can lead to taking on other people's feelings and problems or to being overwhelmed by your own emotions. It affects energy assimilation and utilization. Emotional ''hooks' from other people can be found here.

Negative quality: inferiority. *Positive quality:* emotional stability.

Heart chakra (over your heart)

The sphere of love and nurturing. If your heart chakra is blocked, love cannot flourish, feelings such as jealousy are common and there is enormous resistance to change.

Negative quality: possessiveness. *Positive quality:* peaceful harmony.

Higher heart chakra (thymus)

(between the heart and the throat)

The sphere of compassion. If this chakra is blocked, unconditional love and service cannot be offered. You will be emotionally needy and unable to express feelings openly. *Negative quality:* neediness. *Positive quality:* unconditional love.

Throat chakra (the centre of your throat)

The sphere of communication. If this chakra is blocked, your thoughts and feelings cannot be verbalized. Other people's opinions can cause you difficulties.

Negative quality: mendacity. *Positive quality:* truthful self-expression.

Brow chakra (third eye)

(above and between your eyebrows)

The sphere of intuition and mental connection. Imbalances here can create a sense of your being bombarded by other people's thoughts, or being overtaken by wild and irrational intuitions that have no basis in truth. Controlling or coercing mental 'hooks' from other people can lock in here and affect your thoughts.

Negative quality: delusion. *Positive quality:* intuitive insight.

Crown chakra (top of your head)

The sphere of spiritual communication and awareness. If the crown chakra is blocked, attempting to control others is common, and if it is stuck open, obsession and openness to spiritual interference or possession can result.

Negative quality: arrogance. *Positive quality:* spirituality.

Higher crown chakras (above your head)

The sphere of service and spiritual enlightenment. If these chakras are stuck open, you are spaced out and open to delusion. Influence from other realms of being and entity attachment is possible.

Negative quality: spiritually untrustworthy. *Positive quality:* enlightenment.

Additional chakras

In addition, two other chakras are often involved in the subtle causes of dis-ease, and may underlie some chronic illnesses, especially immune deficiencies or malfunctions:

Spleen chakra (below left armpit)

The sphere of assertion and empowerment. If this chakra is imbalanced, you will have anger issues or suffer constant irritation, with your body turning in to attack itself. If the chakra is too open, other people can draw on your energy, leaving you depleted particularly at the immune level.

Negative quality: aggression. *Positive quality:* self-assertive and empowered.

Past-life chakras (three fingers breadth behind your ears, just above the bony ridge)

The sphere of memory and hereditary issues. Imbalances mean that you are stuck in the past and cannot move forward, and may well be repeating your own past life patterns or ancestral patterns that have passed down through your family. This is also a point where people from the past can attach and control you.

Negative quality: dependence. *Positive quality:* self-directed.

HEALING PLACEMENTS

When placing out stones for your own healing, or that of other people, the crystals can be positioned on or around the body. Some stones work best in contact with the skin but most can be placed over clothes. Many stones are beneficial when left in place for long periods of time, overnight for example, but all can provide benefit from being left in place, or being held, for about 20 to 30 minutes (dowse to ascertain the exact time, and are most effective when you are in a relaxed state. It is, therefore, more important that you are comfortable than that you carry out a placement exactly as shown. If lying on your back is uncomfortable, for instance, and is not alleviated by placing a pillow under your knees, by all means sit in a chair. The stones can always be taped in place.

When you have placed the stones, close your eyes and breathe gently and evenly and allow yourself to relax and feel the energy of the crystal radiating out through your whole being.

The placements that follow can be adapted for any condition or situation.

Chakra rebalancer

Place a stone of the appropriate colour (see page 15) on each chakra and leave in place for 20–30 minutes.

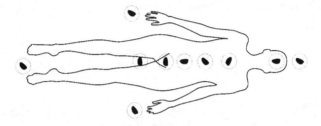

Immune stimulator

Place Bloodstone over the thymus (higher heart chakra) and leave in place for 20–30 minutes. This placement can be greatly enhanced by the use of other immune system crystals (see page 112 in the directory) such as Smithsonite, placed at intervals around the body

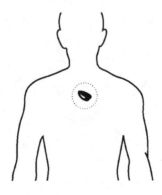

Headache release

Sit or lie quietly with one of the headache or migraine crystals (see page 108 in the directory) on the forehead, temples or base of the neck if the headache radiates from that point. Leave in place for 20–30 minutes.

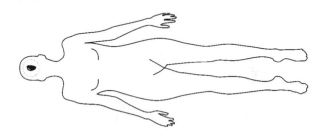

Pain release and organ healer

Place one of the pain relief or organ crystals over the site of the pain or organ for as long as possible. If the problem lies with one of the organs of the body, place the appropriate stone directly over the organ or on the chakra associated with it.

Emotional or mental soother

Sit holding an appropriate crystal – which can be placed against the chakra connected to the problem – while concentrating on breathing deeply and evenly. Picture the troublesome emotion or mental problem flowing into the earth beneath your feet and being replaced by soothing energy from the crystal.

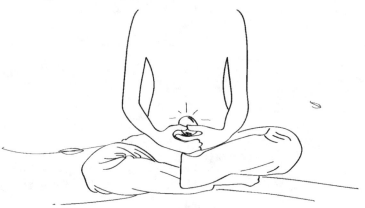

Insomnia release

Place crystals for insomnia (see page 114 in the directory) under your pillow at night. Additional crystals can be added underneath the corners of your mattress or placed around the four corners of the room if outside influences are creating the problem. If the insomnia arises from geopathic stress (see page 104), electromagnetic pollution (see page 94), psychic attack (see page 142), stomach upset (see page 155), or over-thinking (see page 134), use appropriate crystals for the underlying cause (you may need to dowse for this, see page 22).

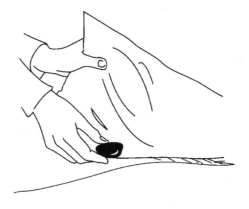

Soothing a child

Place four large pieces of Rose Quartz or Selenite close to the corners of the bed or cot. If the child is old enough, place the crystal under the pillow. If night terrors or nightmares are causing a problem, use appropriate stones (see nightmares, page 132 in the directory, and calming fear, page 77).

Earth healing or electromagnetic pollution blocker

Place a Brown Aragonite, Black Tourmaline, Smoky Quartz or Selenite at each of the four corners of your property or in any room that feels particularly affected by adverse energy, and leave in place permanently. Dowse to see whether additional placements are necessary.

Crystals that are best placed directly on the skin

Crystals with points	Bloodstone
Kunzite	Azurite with Malachite (polished stone)
Fuchsite	
Muscovite	Yellow Labradorite
Malachite (polished stone)	Pyrolusite
	Chrysocolla
Lepidolite	Amber
Topaz	Chrysoberyl
Emerald	Morganite
Sapphire	Rutilated Quartz
Magnesite	Turquoise
Magnetite	Jade
Pearl	Kyanite
Selenite	Sodalite
Tourmaline	Apophyllite
Moss Agate	Danburite

CRYSTAL REMEDIES

Crystal remedies are an excellent way to use the healing power of crystals, and several crystals can be combined provided you dowse to check compatibility. The remedies are ideally suited to children as they can be gently rubbed on the skin or sprayed into a room. Remedies intended for adult use are usually added to a glass of water and sipped, or taken from a dropper bottle.

Crystal remedies are made by transferring the subtle energies and minute concentrations of the mineral constituents of the crystal into water, which then stores the vibrations and transfers them to the physical or subtle bodies in exactly the same way that a homoeopathic remedy works. The remedy is bottled and a preservative – brandy, vodka or cider vinegar – added.

Some stones, such as Malachite, Sulphur, Galena and Vanadinite, are toxic and remedies from these stones need to be made by an indirect method that transfers the vibrations without transferring any of the toxic material from which the stone is formed. If in doubt, make the remedy by the indirect method, which is also suitable for fragile or layered stones. If the remedy is to be taken internally by children or those with an aversion to alcohol, cider vinegar can be used as a preservative.

MAKING A CRYSTAL REMEDY

All you need to make a crystal remedy is the appropriate crystal, which has been cleansed and purified (see pages 28–30), one or two clean glass bowls, spring water and a suitable bottle in which to keep it (coloured glass is preferable to clear as it preserves the vibrations better). Remedies can be made by the direct or indirect method. Spring water should be used rather than tap water that has chlorine, fluoride and aluminium added to it. Water from a spring with healing properties is particularly effective.

Direct method

Place enough spring water in a glass bowl to cover the crystal. Stand the bowl in sunlight for several hours. (If the bowl is left outside, cover with a glass lid or clingfilm to prevent insects falling into it.) If appropriate, the bowl can also be left overnight in moonlight.

Indirect method

Place the crystal in a small glass bowl and stand the bowl within a large bowl that has sufficient spring water to raise the level above the crystal in the inner bowl. Stand the bowl in sunlight for several hours. (If the bowl is left outside, cover with a glass lid or clingfilm.) If appropriate, the bowl can also be left overnight in moonlight.

Bottling and preserving

If the remedy is not to be used within a day, top up with two-thirds brandy, vodka or cider vinegar to one-third remedy, otherwise the remedy will become musty. This makes a 'mother remedy' that can be further diluted. To make a small dosage bottle, add seven drops of the mother remedy to a dosage bottle containing two-thirds brandy and one-third water. If a spray bottle is being made, add seven drops of mother remedy to pure water if using immediately. For prolonged use, vodka makes a useful preservative as it has no smell.

Using a crystal remedy

For short-term use, a remedy can be sipped every few minutes or rubbed on the affected part. Hold the water in your mouth for a few moments. If a dropper bottle has been made, drop seven drops under your tongue at regular intervals until the symptoms or condition ceases.

Remedies can also be applied to the skin, either at the wrist or over the site of a problem, or added to bath water.

If a spray bottle is made, spray all around the aura or around the room. This is particularly effective for clearing negative energies, especially from a sickroom or an electromagnetically or emotionally stressed place.

USING THIS DIRECTORY

In the directory you will find an A–Z list of symptoms and common ailments that may occur physically, emotionally or mentally; together with a list of useful stones for improving vitality, fostering positive emotions and such like. Crystals that are particularly recommended are underlined, but most symptoms have several crystals listed that would be beneficial, although a few have only one. There is a choice because everyone is subtly different and deeper causes will underlie a symptom. Crystals heal holistically – that is to say they work at a causal level on the whole person. What works for you will not necessarily work for your friend because you will have different causes for your dis-ease and may well have different body types.

Many of the entries also have a chakra or chakras associated with them. This means that the condition can be treated through putting appropriate stones on the chakra and leaving in place for 20 minutes or so.

To identify the right crystal, check out your symptom – or symptoms. If you have several, you may well find that one crystal is beneficial for all. This will be the crystal for you. It could be that you already own a crystal, having been instinctively drawn to it. But you may be left with a choice of several crystals, in which case turn to page 27 to learn how to identify the one that will be of greatest benefit to you, although many crystals work well in combination. In a few cases you will find a prescription included, such as Azurite with Malachite, as the two or three stones included support and work with each other (you can either look for a combination stone, or use the individual stones together). Occasionally certain crystals are contra-indicated and you will find these listed in the directory under Contra-indications (page 85).

WOULD AN EXAMPLE OR TWO HELP?

Finding your own crystal prescription can appear daunting if you are new to this. But it needn't be. Dowsing really is the simplest way to choose your stones (see pages 24–26), but you may want to do it more systematically. Many of the stones work well in combination, so let's look at a few examples and different ways of doing things.

Hayley has a problem with repetitive strain injury caused by moving her computer mouse constantly. She looks up **repetitive strain injury** in the directory and finds Fuchsite or Muscovite listed. She places a flat slab of Fuchsite, a pretty, pearly stone a friend had given her, on the mouse mat as a wrist-support and finds that the pain disappears within 24 hours. She continues to use the stone as a wrist support to prevent a recurrence.

Anne can't sleep at night. When she does eventually drop off, she jolts awake after just an hour or two, dozes fitfully, but then wakes again, and so it goes on. During the day she feels slightly nauseous, spaced out and headachy, a feeling that worsens when she gets home from work. She looks up **insomnia** and finger dowses for the cause of her problem. She finds that both **geopathic/electromagnetic stress** and **negative environmental influences** are strongly indicated. Interestingly, a new mast near by has been the subject of controversy in her village as campaigners have been worried about its effect on health. Dowsing confirms that Black Tourmaline around the corners of her bedroom would be beneficial, and around the corners of the house as well. She then turns to **headaches** and Smoky Quartz is indicated. Dowsing to see how she should use this stone, she finds that lying for 20 minutes before bedtime with the Smoky Quartz point up on her forehead would be beneficial. At her local crystal store, she buys eight Black Tourmalines half the size of her thumb, and a small, lightish-coloured Smoky Quartz with a wide flat side. This stone isn't much to look at but it 'speaks' to Anne immediately and her hand tingles when she picks it up. That night, she sleeps through until morning. After a week she no longer needs the Smoky Quartz daily, but uses it once a week as a precautionary measure.

Peter is, like many men, overworked and overstretched. So when he gets home at night, he likes a drink or three to relax with. He decides to turn to crystals to help him before it becomes a real problem. So he looks up **alcohol** in the directory and finds an entry for **mitigate the effects of** with two crystals listed: Iolite and Amethyst. He notices **alcoholism** underneath and although he doesn't think he's got to this stage yet, he can see that Amethyst is good here too. This is a stone he recognizes and can pick up in any crystal shop – and he even thinks he's seen one at home, although as it's a cluster it might be rather large for healing purposes, but he could keep it on his desk so it radiates its healing vibes out to him. So that's where he'll start. But he notices that Iolite also comes under **addictive behaviour, understand the reasons for** and he files that away for future reference.

Peter's pretty sure that his liver is affected by his drinking – he feels 'liverish' and hung over in the mornings, but he's not sure exactly where his liver is. Right side, left side? Above the waist, below the waist? Fortunately he can turn to page xx to check out exactly where his liver lives (on the right side of his body roughly between his right nipple and his waist, although it's a bit of an odd shape as he can see). He turns to **liver** in the directory and finds a wealth of crystals that could help him. Should he use Yellow Jasper, which is underlined as being very beneficial for the liver, or should he turn to **damage due to alcohol**, or **detoxifying**? At this point, dowsing would help him, but Peter is determined to reason this through. He remembers seeing the chakra diagram on page 37 and turns to this for help. But does his problem stem from the solar plexus chakra or the sacral? He feels that lack of self-worth probably underlies his drinking, which is sacral, but a feeling of inferiority probably fits in too and the solar plexus is closer to the liver than the sacral. This means yellow stones are good for him, so the Yellow Jasper he spotted earlier could be beneficial. He decides to give it a go, but to support the detoxification with Malachite. Not sure what Malachite looks like, he turns to a website for clarification. Here he finds a beautifully veined, vivid green stone that reminds him of a labyrinth. But the site is asking $70 and he realizes it's a huge stone that wouldn't feel comfortable on his liver, or his pocket. So he pops into his local crystal store. As he walks in the door, he is attracted to a piece of polished Malachite, just the right size to sit in his hand, or over his liver. Playing with a bowl of mottled yellow stones on the counter, he is not surprised to see them labelled as Yellow Jasper. One sticks to his fingers and this is the one he buys to keep in his right-hand shirt pocket to support his liver. Talking to the storekeeper, he mentions Chrysoberyl, which she confirms is an excellent stone for enhancing self-worth. She promises to give him a call when she gets some in, explaining that it's often faceted and set as jewellery. A few weeks later, Peter is wearing his Chrysoberyl and Yellow Jasper constantly, the Chrysoberyl on a chain around his neck and the Yellow Jasper taped over his solar plexus every night and in his shirt pocket during the day. He lies down and relaxes every evening for 20 minutes with the Malachite over his liver. And he realizes that he has not yet reached for the bottle.

Note for chocolate addicts – this course of action will work for you, too!

INSTRUCTION FOR USE

Instructions for use are given after some of the directory entries. Instructions given at the end of a list of crystals apply to the whole list, for example (Wear continuously). Instructions given after a specific crystal apply only to that crystal, for example Sulphur (use as polished stone).

PART II

DIRECTORY OF
SYMPTOMS

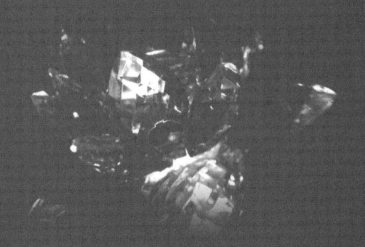

- A -

Abandonment, overcome feelings of: pink stones, Dioptase, Lavender-pink Smithsonite, Sunstone. *Chakra:* base, heart

Abdomen: orange stones, Fire Opal, Smoky Quartz, Atacamite. *Chakra:* sacral

Abdominal distension or colic: Aragonite (White), Carnelian, Variscite, Snowflake Obsidian. *Chakra:* sacral

Accepting oneself: Chrysoprase, Rhodochrosite. *Chakra:* sacral, heart

Abortion, healing after: Wulfenite. *Chakra:* sacral

Absorption of nutrients, see Assimilation, *Chakra:* solar plexus

Abuse: Rhodonite, Red Calcite, Carnelian. *Chakra:* base, sacral

> **emotional:** Smithsonite. *Chakra:* sacral, heart
> **sexual:** Rhodochrosite, Pink Carnelian. *Chakra:* base, sacral

Acceptance of physical body: Vanadinite (make remedy by indirect method), Phenacite. *Chakra:* earth, base, crown

Accidents, prevention of: Carnelian (carry at all times or keep in car)

Unless otherwise directed, apply crystal over organ or site of symptom, place on appropriate chakra, wear as jewellery, bathe with or take as crystal remedy.

Acidity: Green Jasper, Peridot

Aches and pains: <u>Cathedral Quartz</u> on site of pain, Quartz, Charoite, Magnetite (Lodestone), Rose Quartz, Hematite, Yellow Jasper

Acid: Green Jasper, Diamond

    acid/alkaline imbalance: Jade

    acidification of tissue: Malachite (use as polished stone, make remedy by indirect method)

    correct overacidification: Bloodstone, Diamond, Chiastolite, Green Jasper, Malachite (use as polished stone, make remedy by indirect method), Turquoise, Variscite, Zoisite, Pearl

    acidosis: Uvarovite Garnet (take as crystal remedy)

    indigestion: Pearl (take as crystal remedy)

Acne: Amethyst, Idocrase. (Bathe with crystal remedy or apply stone to skin)

Addictions: <u>Amber</u>, <u>Amethyst</u>, Black Onyx, Dioptase, Kunzite, Lepidolite, Lavender-pink Smithsonite, Phenacite, Tourmaline with Lepidolite, Peridot. (Take as alcohol-free remedy or carry at all times.)

Addictive behaviour:

    overcome: Tiger's Eye (carry at all times). *Chakra:* base

    understand reasons for: Iolite (place on base or solar plexus chakra). *Chakra:* base

Adhesions: Fluorite

Unless otherwise directed, apply crystal over organ or site of symptom, place on appropriate chakra, wear as jewellery, bathe with or take as crystal remedy.

Adrenal glands: Aventurine. *Chakra:* solar plexus

  balancing: Fire Opal, Yellow Labradorite, Rose Quartz

  calming: Green Calcite, Kyanite

  stimulating: Sugilite

Adverse environmental factors: Smoky Quartz, Black Tourmaline, Aragonite, Amazonite, Malachite (use as polished stone, make remedy by indirect method). (Place crystal or apply remedy at four corners of house or site, place on computer etc.) *Chakra:* earth

Age spots: Selenite (rub gently with crystal or apply remedy made by indirect method or from a polished stone)

Ageing, retarding: Rhodochrosite, Sapphire, Sodalite, Pearl, Diamond, Sodalite. (Wear or bathe in crystal remedy)

Aggression:

  ameliorate: <u>Bloodstone</u>, Carnelian, Amethyst, Rose Quartz, Ruby. *Chakra:* base

  use positively: Ruby Aura Quartz. *Chakra:* base

Alcohol, mitigate effects of: Iolite, Amethyst. (Use as alcohol-free crystal remedy or carry stone)

Alcoholism: <u>Amethyst</u> (wear constantly), Black Onyx, Smithsonite. *Chakra:* base

Alienation, overcome: Andradite Garnet. *Chakra:* earth, solar plexus

---

Unless otherwise directed, apply crystal over organ or site of symptom, place on appropriate chakra, wear as jewellery, bathe with or take as crystal remedy.

Align:

> **physical, emotional, mental subtle bodies:** Alexandrite, Zincite. *Chakra:* all
>
> **the chakras:** see pages 79–81

AIDS: Ametrine, Lapis Lazuli, Jadeite, Petalite, Zincite

Allergies: Apophyllite, Danburite, Iolite, Lepidolite, Muscovite, Aquamarine, Zircon, Carnelian, Red Jasper, Chrysoprase, Cat's Eye (Carry crystal.)

Altitude sickness: Cuprite

Alzheimers: Blue Obsidian, Lepidolite, Rose Quartz, Kunzite, Rutilated Quartz, Purple Tourmaline. (Take as crystal remedy or wear constantly.) *Chakra:* brow

Anaemia: <u>Bloodstone</u>, <u>Ruby</u>, Hematite, Citrine, Kunzite, Tiger's Eye, Tourmaline, Garnet, Carnelian. *Chakra:* heart, spleen

Anaesthetic, neutralize effects of: Amber, Kunzite. (Hold)

Ancestral line, healing: Bloodstone, Black Obsidian, Petalite, Tibetan Turquoise. *Chakra:* past life, base

Anger, ameliorate: Blue Lace Agate, Carnelian, Amethyst, Muscovite, Rose Quartz, Peridot. *Chakra:* base

Angina: <u>Rhodonite</u>, Amethyst, Candle Quartz, Dioptase, Emerald, Rose Quartz, Magnesite, Rhodochrosite. *Chakra:* heart, base

Animals:

    heal: Dioptase

    calm: Dalmation Jasper

Anorexia: Ametrine, Lepidolite, Topaz, Rhodochrosite, Rose Quartz, Stibnite. *Chakra:* earth, base, heart

Antibacterial: Iolite, Amber. (Bathe in crystal remedy or apply stone.)

Anti-inflammatory: <u>Moss Agate</u>, <u>Magnetite (Lodestone)</u>, Blue Chalcedony, Turquoise. (Wear constantly.) *Chakra:* base

Antiseptic: Amethyst, Calcite, Amber. (Bathe in crystal remedy or apply stone.)

Antispasmodic: Aragonite, Magnesite, Azurite

Anti-viral: Fluorite

Anxiety: <u>Kunzite</u>, Aventurine, Green Calcite, Chrysoprase, Emerald, Hematite, Moonstone, Pyrite, Rose Quartz, Rutilated Quartz, Smithsonite, Tiger's Eye, Tourmaline, Labradorite. *Chakra:* earth, base

Apathy: Red Calcite. *Chakra:* base, sacral

Aphrodisiac: red stones, Amethyst, Carnelian, Rose Quartz, Pink Tourmaline, Red Jasper. *Chakra:* base, sacral

Apoplexy: Ametrine. *Chakra:* heart

Appendix: Peridot, Yellow Sapphire

Appetite suppressant: Apatite. *Chakra:* solar plexus

Arms: Malachite (use as polished stone, make remedy by

Unless otherwise directed, apply crystal over organ or site of symptom, place on appropriate chakra, wear as jewellery, bathe with or take as crystal remedy.

indirect method), Jadeite

Arteries:

> **blocked:** Larimar, Obsidian. *Chakra:* heart

> **strengthen:** Bloodstone, Stibnite

Arteriosclerosis: Aventurine, Magnesite

Arthritis: <u>Fluorite</u>, Apatite, Amethyst, Azurite, Blue Lace Agate, Carnelian, Chrysocolla, Green Calcite, Garnet, Hematite, Malachite (use as polished stone, make remedy by indirect method), Obsidian (wear for short periods only), Rhodonite (see also joints and pain relief)

Ascension process, assist: Kyanite. *Chakra:* higher crown

Assertion: red stones, Fire Agate. *Chakra:* base, sacral

Assimilation:

> **of calcium:** Honey Calcite, Howlite. *Chakra:* solar plexus

> **of iron:** Blue Opal, Chrysocolla. *Chakra:* solar plexus

> **of nutrients:** Turquoise. *Chakra:* solar plexus

> **of oxygen:** Botswana Agate, Fluorite. *Chakra:* solar plexus

> **of protein:** Opal. *Chakra:* solar plexus

> **of vitamin C:** Chrysoprase, Chrysocolla. *Chakra:* solar plexus

Asthma: <u>Apophyllite</u>, <u>Amber</u>, Amethyst, Ametrine, Dark-blue Sapphire, Iron Pyrite, Malachite (use as polished stone, make remedy by indirect method), Morganite,

Magnetite (Lodestone), Rose Quartz, Rhodochrosite, Tiger's Eye, Vanadinite (make remedy by indirect method), Topaz, Chrysoberyl. (Wear constantly over chest, take as crystal remedy.) *Chakra:* solar plexus, higher heart

Astigmatism: Peridot (bathe eyes in alcohol-free crystal remedy, wear as earrings)

Astral projection: Calcite, Double-terminated crystals, Hematite, Kunzite, Muscovite, Kyanite. *Chakra:* brow, crown

> **facilitate:** double-terminated crystals, Muscovite. (Hold or apply to brow chakra)
>
> **protection during:** Fluorite. (Hold or wear)
>
> **prevention:** Angelite (Wear constantly at night or place by bed)

Astringent: Emerald

Atmospheric pollutants: Turquoise, Smoky Quartz, Black Tourmaline. (Place in environment to absorb or wear.) *Chakra:* earth

Atrophy: Septarian, Blue or Yellow Sapphire

Attitude, to change: Agate, Aventurine, Fluorite, Obsidian (use sparingly, see Contra-indications. *Chakra:* as appropriate.

Aura: Quartz (Hold in front of solar plexus). *Chakra:* all
> **align with physical body:** Amber (Hold over head or solar plexus)

Unless otherwise directed, apply crystal over organ or site of symptom, place on appropriate chakra, wear as jewellery, bathe with or take as crystal remedy.

align with spiritual energy: Labradorite (Hold over crown chakra)

cleansing: <u>Smoky Quartz</u>, <u>Quartz</u>, Amber, Bloodstone, Green Jasper, Quartz, Herkimer Diamond ('Comb' aura thoroughly.)

energize: <u>Quartz</u>, Iolite. *Chakra:* solar plexus

energy leakage, guard against: Labradorite (Wear constantly). *Chakra:* higher heart

entities, remove: <u>Smoky Amethyst</u>, Kunzite and Selenite, Petalite, Fairy Quartz. *Chakra:* base, sacral, solar plexus, brow

'holes': <u>Quartz</u>, Aqua Aura, Amethyst, Green Tourmaline, Quartz (Place over site.)

mental attachments, remove: Kunzite and Selenite, Petalite. (Place on chakra until released, then purify immediately.) *Chakra:* brow

negativity, remove: Black Jade, Amber, Apache Tear (Hold crystal over solar plexus.)

negative patterns embedded in, dissolve: Smoky Quartz ('Comb' over aura)

protecting: <u>Apache Tear</u>, <u>Labradorite</u>, <u>Shattuckite with Ajoite</u>, Amber, Amethyst, Diamond, Quartz. (Wear continuously.) *Chakra:* higher heart

stabilize: Agate, Labradorite. *Chakra:* earth

strengthen: Magnetite (Lodestone), Quartz, Zircon

Unless otherwise directed, apply crystal over organ or site of symptom, place on appropriate chakra, wear as jewellery, bathe with or take as crystal remedy.

weakness, overcome: Hiddenite

Autism: <u>Sugilite</u>, Cerussite, Charoite, Moldavite. (Wear continuously or keep in pocket.) *Chakra:* earth, base, solar plexus

Autoimmune diseases: Aquamarine, Rhodonite. *Chakra:* higher heart

Autonomic nervous system: Ametrine, Sunstone

- B -

Babies, enhance physical development: Rhodochrosite, Dioptase, Sodalite, Chrysocolla. *Chakra:* earth, base, sacral

Back:

    pain: <u>Cathedral Quartz</u> (over site of pain), Malachite (use as polished stone, make remedy by indirect method), Magnetite (Lodestone), Sapphire, Lapis Lazuli

    disc elasticity: Aragonite

    impacted vertebrae: Electric-blue Obsidian

Backache: <u>Iolite</u>, <u>Amber</u>, Cathedral Quartz, Sapphire, Magnetite, Blue Agate, Hematite

Bacterial infections: Blue Tourmaline, Green Calcite. (Bathe in crystal remedy or place stone over site.)

Bad:

    breath: Sunstone

    temper, ameliorate: Bloodstone (wear continuously), Emerald (use as crystal remedy)

Baggage, releasing emotional: pink stones, Beryl, Peridot, Obsidian. *Chakra:* solar plexus, heart

Balance: Sugilite

    male/female energies: Tourmalinated Quartz, Green

Tourmaline, Hematite with Rutile (Place over sacral chakra.)

mineral content: Red or Yellow Jasper. (Place over solar plexus)

physical body: Amazonite (Wear continuously)

yin–yang: Celestite, Black Onyx, Citrine, Hematite, Merlinite. (Wear or place over sacral chakra.)

Baldness: Aquamarine (see Hair)

Base chakra: red stones, see Chakras

Bedsores: Amethyst, Blue Lace Agate, Ruby

Belching: Beryl (Place over heart chakra)

Benevolence, enhance: Jade (Wear continuously)

Beta brain waves: Double-terminated Violet Amethyst. *Chakra:* brow, crown

Bigotry, overcome effects of: Chrysanthemum Stone. *Chakra:* heart

Bile duct blockages: Red Jasper, Emerald

Biliousness: yellow stones, Emerald. *Chakra:* solar plexus

Biomagnetic field destabilized: Quartz, Kyanite, Magnetite (Lodestone) *Chakra:* solar plexus

Biorhythmic clock: Moonstone. *Chakra:* higher heart

Bi-polar disorder: Charoite, Kunzite, Larimar, Peridot. *Chakra:* brow

Birth: Moss Agate, Lapis Lazuli, Opal, Carnelian. (Bind over abdomen.) *Chakra:* sacral

Unless otherwise directed, apply crystal over organ or site of symptom, place on appropriate chakra, wear as jewellery, bathe with or take as crystal remedy.

birth canal, opening: Peridot

pain, lessen: Moss Agate

(and see Childbirth)

Bites, venomous: Sulphur (use as polished crystallized stone, make remedy by indirect method), Emerald, Sard (Apply to site.)

Blackouts: Lapis Lazuli

Bladder: Amber, Jade, Red Jasper, Prehnite, Vanadinite (make remedy by indirect method), Topaz, Jasper, Orange Calcite, Bloodstone, Tourmaline, Yellow Sapphire

    stones: Green Jasper

Bleeding: <u>Ruby</u>, <u>Bloodstone,</u> Carnelian, Topaz, Sapphire

    cauterize/stop: Bloodstone, Ruby, Sapphire. (Apply over site.)

    excessive: Carnelian, Chiastolite, Red Chalcedony, Obsidian, Ruby, Shattuckite

    nose: Topaz

    menstrual, excessive: Carnelian, Jasper

Blisters: Quartz, Blue Lace Agate, Rose Quartz. (Bathe in crystal remedy or apply stone.)

Bloating: Green Jasper, Zeolite

Blockages, self-imposed, arising out of fear or excessive caution: Larimar. *Chakra:* higher heart

Blood: red stones. *Chakra:* heart, spleen

    cells, red to white ratio: Fuchsite, Tiger Iron

clots: Bloodstone, Hematite, Amethyst

circulation: Sodalite, Carnelian, Galena (make remedy by indirect method), Seraphinite, Pink Tourmaline, Ruby, Bloodstone, Amethyst

cleanser: <u>Hematite</u>, <u>Bloodstone</u>, Amethyst, Ametrine, Aquamarine, Garnet, Mookaite, Lapis Lazuli, Ruby, Tourmaline. *Chakra:* spleen

clots, dissolve: Amethyst, Bloodstone, Hematite

clotting, improve: Calcite, Red Chalcedony, Sapphire, Shattuckite

disorders: Amethyst, Bloodstone, Chrysocolla, Cherry Opal, Lapis Lazuli, Mookaite, Blue Quartz, Sapphire, Magnetite (Lodestone), Onyx, Prehnite

excessive clotting: Magnesite

faulty oxygenation: Amethyst, Carnelian, Chrysocolla

flow in liver: Albite, Variscite, Mookaite

poisoning: Carnelian

purification: Pink Tourmaline, Bloodstone, Angelite, Sapphire

sugar: Muscovite

vessels: Fluorite, Topaz

Blood pressure:

equalize: Aventurine, Tourmaline, Charoite. *Chakra:* heart

high: Blue Chalcedony, Amethyst, Bloodstone,

Unless otherwise directed, apply crystal over organ or site of symptom, place on appropriate chakra, wear as jewellery, bathe with or take as crystal remedy.

Dioptase, Charoite, Chrysocolla, Emerald, Jade, Kyanite, Labradorite, Lapis Lazuli, Malachite (use as polished stone, make remedy by indirect method), Rhodochrosite, Sodalite, Dioptase, Chrysoprase. *Chakra:* heart

low: Carnelian, Red Calcite, Sodalite, Tourmaline, Rhodochrosite, Ruby. *Chakra:* heart

Blood sugar imbalances: Muscovite, Peridot. *Chakra:* spleen

Blood vessels, weak: Pyrolusite, Chrysocolla

Body:

discomfort at being in: Vanadinite (make remedy by indirect method), Phenacite. *Chakra:* earth, base, sacral

fluids: Sardonyx, Halite. *Chakra:* earth, base, sacral

heat, excess: Hematite. *Chakra:* earth, base, sacral

odour: Magnesite, Orbicular Jasper. *Chakra:* earth, base, sacral

promote repair: Apatite. *Chakra:* earth, base, sacral

strengthen: Agate, Amazonite. *Chakra:* earth, base, sacral

Boils: Amber, Idocrase, Sapphire, Lapis Lazuli

Bombarded by other people's thoughts: Azurite, Labradorite, Quartz. (Wear continuously.) *Chakra:* brow

Bones:

aching: Cathedral Quartz, Magnetite (Lodestone),

Spinel, Rose Quartz

broken: Malachite (use as polished stone, make remedy by indirect method), Apatite, Hematite, Magnesite

disease: Chrysocolla, Tiger's Eye

disorders: Chrysocolla, Magnesite, Topaz, Tourmaline

growth: Rhodonite, Calcite

healing: Apatite, Iron Pyrite, Onyx, Rutilated Quartz

marrow: Amber, Chalcedony, Purple Fluorite, Lapis Lazuli, Onyx

strengthening: Fluorite, Selenite, Desert Rose, Topaz, Tourmaline, Chrysocolla

structure: Howlite, Calcite

Bone-marrow disorders: Violet-purple Fluorite, Lapis Lazuli, Onyx

Boundaries, weak: Red Jasper, Quartz. (Wear continuously.) *Chakra:* solar plexus

Bowels: Hawk's Eye, Jasper (especially Yellow), Tourmaline

Brain: Amber, Amethyst, Beryl, Botswana Agate, Carnelian, Green Tourmaline, Kyanite, Labradorite, Magnesite, Royal Sapphire, Staurolite. *Chakra:* brow, crown

balance left–right hemispheres: Sugilite, Hematite with Rutile

blood flow, improve: Iron Pyrite

damage: Thulite, Zircon, Lapis Lazuli

detox: Ruby

disorders: Stillbite, Sapphire

fatigue: Turquoise

frequencies: Lavender Quartz

stimulate activity: Larimar, Lapis Lazuli

tumour: Emerald

Brave face, always puts on: Hiddenite. *Chakra:* solar plexus

Breastfeeding: <u>Moonstone</u>, Chiastolite, Okenite, Pink Chalcedony, Selenite

Breathlessness: <u>Amber</u>, <u>Apophyllite,</u> Amethyst, Jet, Magnetite (Lodestone), Morganite, Moss Agate, Black Onyx, Vanadinite (make remedy by indirect method). *Chakra:* solar plexus, throat

Breathing disorders: Vanadinite (make remedy by indirect method), Moss Agate, Morganite

Bronchitis: <u>Amber</u>, Black Onyx, Iron Pyrite, Pyrolusite, Rutilated Quartz, Jet

Bruises: Amethyst, Blue Lace Agate, Hematite and Rose Quartz

Brow chakra: indigo stones, see Chakras

Bulimia: Rose Quartz, Stibnite. *Chakra:* solar plexus

Burning sensation: Ametrine

Burn-out: Fire Opal, Quartz. *Chakra:* sacral

Burns: <u>Quartz</u>, <u>Rose Quartz</u>, Amethyst, Blue Tourmaline,

Chrysoprase, Chrysocolla, Jadeite, Sodalite, Moonstone.
(Place stone in cold water and immerse burn for 20
minutes.)

Bursitis: Amber, Blue Lace Agate

- C -

Calcification: Aragonite, Calcite, Garnet, Malachite (use as polished stone, make remedy by indirect method), Pearl

Calcium:

    absorption: Apatite. *Chakra:* solar plexus

    deficiency: Amazonite, Sodalite, Thulite, Pearl

    excess: Peridot

    imbalances: Howlite, Serpentine, Spessarite

Calcium–magnesium balance: Yellow Kunzite, Serpentine. *Chakra:* solar plexus

Calming: pink or green stones. *Chakra:* heart, solar plexus

    emotional: Sugilite, Amethyst, Aquamarine, Calcite, Carnelian, Chrysocolla, Citrine, Fuchsite, Kunzite, Opal, Prehnite, Rhodochrosite, Rhodonite, Rose Quartz, Selenite, Variscite

    fear: Moss Agate, Smoky Quartz

    mental: Blue Calcite, Petalite

    physical: Amethyst

Cancer: Amethyst, Azeztulite, Carnelian, Magnetite (Lodestone) with Smoky Quartz, Melanite Garnet, Petalite, Red Jasper, Smoky Quartz, Sugilite

    support during: Sugilite

Unless otherwise directed, apply crystal over organ or site of symptom, place on appropriate chakra, wear as jewellery, bathe with or take as crystal remedy.

skin: Amethyst, Emerald

Cancerous growths (see also Tumours): Amethyst

Candida: Carnelian, Zincite

Capillaries: Dendritic Agate

Capillary degeneration: Dendritic Agate, Tektite

Carbohydrate assimilation: Staurolite *Chakra:* solar plexus

Carbuncle: Sapphire (tape over site)

Cardiovascular system: Kunzite, Peridot (and see Heart)

Carpal tunnel syndrome: Fuchsite, Magnetite (Lodestone)

Cataracts: Turquoise (bathe with alcohol-free crystal remedy)

Catarrh: Amber, Blue Agate, Topaz, Sapphire

Cartilage: Apatite, Aragonite, Dalmation Jasper, Larimar

Causes of disease:

> **anxiety or fear:** see appropriate entry
>
> **damaged immune system:** see Immune system
>
> **emotional exhaustion:** see Emotional exhaustion
>
> **negative attitudes or emotions:** see appropriate entry
>
> **shock, trauma or psychic attack:** see appropriate entry
>
> **stress and tension:** see Relaxation and appropriate entries
>
> **underlying, discover:** Blue Tourmaline, Quartz

Cauterization: Ruby

Cell metabolism: Sardonyx

Cell phones, protection against: Black Tourmaline,

Amazonite, Diamond, Smoky Quartz. (Tape to phone.)

Cell rejuvenation: Jasper, Sodalite, Rhodonite

Cellular:

    blueprint: Yellow Kunzite. *Chakra:* higher heart

    disorders: Celestite, Dioptase, Garnet, Herkimer
    Diamond, Iron Pyrite, Yellow Kunzite, Staurolite

    healing: Nebula Stone

    structure: Indicolite, Selenite

Cellulite: Apatite, Citrine

Central nervous system, depleted or disturbed:
Alexandrite, Celestite, Amethyst, Dioptase, Rose Quartz,
Rhodonite, Aventurine. (Wear continuously.)

Cerebellum: Kyanite. *Chakra:* brow, crown

Cervix: Carnelian. *Chakra:* sacral

Chakras:

    align: Kyanite, Citrine, Quartz

    align with physical body: Amber

    balance: Sunstone

    base: red stones, Fire Agate, Garnet, Pink Tourmaline,
    Smoky Quartz, Red Calcite, Red Jasper, Azurite,
    Bloodstone, Chrysocolla, Obsidian, Golden Topaz,
    Black Tourmaline, Carnelian, Citrine, Cuprite

    blockages: Clear Quartz, Lapis Lazuli, Azurite,
    Bloodstone

    blown: Fire Agate (see Chakra Connections)

brow/third eye: indigo stones, Apophyllite, Sodalite, Moldavite, Azurite, Herkimer Diamond, Lapis Lazuli, Garnet, Purple Fluorite, Kunzite, Lepidolite, Malachite with Azurite (use as polished stone, make remedy by indirect method), Royal Sapphire, Electric-blue Obsidian, Yellow Labradorite, Aquamarine, Iolite

cleanse: Amethyst, Quartz, Bloodstone, Calcite, Citrine, Quartz, Tourmaline wand

crown: purple and white stones, Selenite, Angelite, Moldavite, Citrine, Quartz, Red Serpentine, Purple Jasper, Clear Tourmaline, Golden Beryl, Lepidolite, Purple Sapphire, Petalite, Phenacite, Larimar

earth: brown stones, Smoky Quartz, Brown Jasper, Boji Stone, Fire Agate, Brown Jasper, Hematite, Mahogany Obsidian, Tourmaline, Rhodonite, Cuprite

energy leakage, prevent: Labradorite, Ajoite with Shattuckite, Green Aventurine, Quartz

entities, release from: Petalite, Smoky Amethyst

heart: pink or green stones, Rhodonite, Rhodochrosite, Rose Quartz, Green Jasper, Green Quartz, Jadeite, Jade, Aventurine, Kunzite, Variscite, Muscovite, Red Calcite, Watermelon Tourmaline, Pink Tourmaline, Green Tourmaline, Apophyllite, Lepidolite, Morganite, Pink Danburite, Ruby, Chrysocolla, Green Sapphire

higher heart/thymus: pink or green stones, Dioptase,

Kunzite

higher crown: white stones, Petalite, Selenite, Azeztulite, Kunzite, Apophyllite, Celestite, Muscovite, Phenacite

holes, repair: Amethyst, Green Tourmaline, Quartz

mental influences, detach: Kunzite, Selenite

past life: use appropriate crystals from Past-life healing section

negative karma, disturbances from: Petalite

protect: Apache Tear, Jet, Quartz, Labradorite

remove blockages: Azurite, Bloodstone, Lapis Lazuli, Quartz

sacral/navel: orange stones, Orange Calcite, Blue Jasper, Red Jasper, Orange Carnelian, Topaz, Citrine

solar plexus: yellow stones, Malachite (use as polished stone, make remedy by indirect method), Jasper, Tiger's Eye, Citrine, Yellow Tourmaline, Golden Beryl, Rhodochrosite

spleen: Aventurine, Zircon, Ruby, Rhodonite (and see Assertion and Anger)

strengthen: Magnetite (Lodestone), Quartz

throat: blue stones, Azurite, Turquoise, Amethyst, Aquamarine, Blue Topaz, Blue Tourmaline, Amber, Kunzite, Lepidolite, Blue Obsidian, Blue Lace Agate

Unless otherwise directed, apply crystal over organ or site of symptom, place on appropriate chakra, wear as jewellery, bathe with or take as crystal remedy.

Change:

> **facilitating:** Calcite. *Chakra:* heart
>
> **of life:** see Menopause.

Chemotherapy: Smoky Quartz

Chest: Hiddenite, Larimar, Prehnite. *Chakra:* heart

> **constriction:** Chrysopal (Blue-green Opal)
>
> **pains:** Amber, Dioptase, Emerald, Malachite (use as polished stone, make remedy by indirect method), Rose Quartz, Rhodonite, Rhodochrosite

Chickenpox: Azurite, Malachite (use as polished stone, make remedy by indirect method), Topaz, Pearl

Childbirth: Jade, Malachite (use as polished stone, make remedy by indirect method), Moonstone, Opal, Peridot, Wulfenite, Carnelian. *Chakra:* sacral, base

> **ease pain of:** Amber, Cathedral Quartz, Emerald, Lapis Lazuli, Moonstone

Childhood, difficult: Smithsonite. *Chakra:* heart, solar plexus

Chills: Aragonite, Kunzite, Magnesite, Red Tourmaline, Seraphinite

Cholera: Malachite (use as polished stone, make remedy by indirect method)

Cholesterol, high: Aventurine, Magnesite, Yellow Fluorite

Chromosome damage: Chiastolite

Chronic fatigue syndrome: Ametrine, Citrine, Green

Unless otherwise directed, apply crystal over organ or site of symptom, place on appropriate chakra, wear as jewellery, bathe with or take as crystal remedy.

Tourmaline, Zincite (Wear continuously.)

Chronic illness: Danburite, Dendritic Chalcedony, Cat's Eye. *Chakra:* earth, solar plexus, higher heart

Chronic sore throat: Blue Tourmaline, Blue Lace Agate. (Gargle with crystal remedy and wear stone). *Chakra:* throat

Circular breathing: Orbicular Jasper, Vanadinite (make remedy by indirect method)

Circulation: Candle Quartz, Bloodstone, Blue Tiger's Eye, Azurite and Malachite (use as polished stone, make remedy by indirect method), Rhodochrosite, Citrine, Howlite, Rose Quartz, Ruby, Stibnite, Thulite, Yellow Topaz

> **defective:** Diamond
> **fortifying:** Pyrope Garnet
> **poor:** Ruby, Blue John

Circulatory:

> **disorders:** Electric-blue Obsidian, Hawk's Eye, Ruby, Hematite
> **system:** Chalcedony, Iron Pyrite, Jasper, Hematite, Magnetite (Lodestone), Amethyst, Bloodstone, Red Jasper

Clarity, promote: Jade. *Chakra:* brow, crown

Claustrophobia: Chrysoprase, Green Tourmaline, Aventurine. *Chakra:* solar plexus

Cleansing: Peridot, Rose Quartz, Smoky Quartz, Quartz

Unless otherwise directed, apply crystal over organ or site of symptom, place on appropriate chakra, wear as jewellery, bathe with or take as crystal remedy.

aura: Amethyst, Fluorite, Selenite, Quartz. *Chakra:* higher crown.

emotions: Blue Lace Agate, Rhodochrosite. *Chakra:* solar plexus

mind: Azurite. *Chakra:* brow

physical body: Clear Quartz. *Chakra:* earth, base

Clumsiness: Muscovite

Codependence: Chrysoprase, Fuchsite, Iolite. *Chakra:* base.

Colds: Ametrine, Carnelian, Jet, Moss Agate, Emerald, Fluorite, Hyalite, Labradorite, Larimar

Coldness: Citrine, Rose Quartz, Topaz, Opal. *Chakra:* heart

Colic: Malachite (use as polished stone, make remedy by indirect method, apply externally), Jade or Jadeite, Cat's Eye (Place over site of pain.)

Colon: Bloodstone, Carnelian, Citrine, Garnet, Yellow Jasper, Obsidian, Smoky Quartz, Tourmaline. *Chakra:* sacral

Coma: Tanzanite. *Chakra:* crown

Compassion for oneself, lack of: Chrysoprase. *Chakra:* heart

Complexion: Rose Quartz

Compulsions, overcome: Charoite. *Chakra:* base

Computer stress: Amazonite, Lepidolite, Smoky Quartz,

Purple Sugilite. (Place on computer).

Commands to secrecy, release: Shattuckite. *Chakra:* past life

Concentration, improve: Green Tourmaline, Carnelian with Magnetite (Lodestone), Red Jasper. *Chakra:* brow

Conception: Moonstone. *Chakra:* sacral

Concern, alleviate excess: Sodalite. *Chakra:* heart

Concussion: Beryl

Confidence: Agate, Citrine, Galena (make remedy by indirect method), Lapis Lazuli, Rhodonite, Rose Quartz, Ruby, Tourmaline, Variscite. *Chakra:* base

Confusion: Sapphire, Pietersite. *Chakra:* brow

Conjunctivitis: Agate, Blue Sapphire

Connective tissue: Lepidolite, Prehnite

Constipation: Amber, Red Jasper, Citrine, Red Calcite, Ruby, Serpentine, Sunshine Aura Quartz, Green Tourmaline, Ruby. *Chakra:* sacral

Consumption, see Tuberculosis

Contra-indications and cautions:

    aggression, 'macho-men': avoid Iron Pyrite

    delicate people, may overstimulate: Ruby

    depression: avoid Onyx, Obsidian

    during full moon: avoid Moonstone

    energy, scattered: avoid Opal

    Galena: use a polished stone and make crystal remedy

Unless otherwise directed, apply crystal over organ or site of symptom, place on appropriate chakra, wear as jewellery, bathe with or take as crystal remedy.

by indirect method

goitre: avoid Fluorite

heart palpitations, if causes: remove Malachite (use as polished stone, make remedy by indirect method), replace with Rose Quartz or Rhodonite

hysteria: use Moonstone with caution

illusion, may induce: Moonstone

inflammation, do not use when present: Hematite

insomnia/uncontrolled psychic abilities: avoid prolonged wearing of Herkimer Diamond

irritability, may overstimulate: Ruby

Malachite: use polished stone and make crystal remedy by indirect means

negative emotions and unpleasant truths brought to light fast: Obsidian, Opal

negative energy heightened if worn constantly: Emerald

night terrors: avoid Onyx

Obsidian: brings underlying emotions to the surface forcefully. Limit use to 10 minutes a day and apply other crystals as appropriate to support the healing process. Note: Apache Tear is a gentler form of Obsidian and can be used for much longer periods

psychiatric conditions, paranoia or schizophrenia: may be aggravated by: Amethyst

Unless otherwise directed, apply crystal over organ or site of symptom, place on appropriate chakra, wear as jewellery, bathe with or take as crystal remedy.

sleep walking: avoid prolonged wearing: Magnetite (Lodestone), Sapphire, Diamond

Sulphur: use a polished or crystalline stone and make crystal remedy by indirect method

toxic (make crystal remedy by indirect method): Malachite

Vanadinite: make crystal remedy by indirect method

Convalescence: Unakite, Ruby. (Wear constantly)

Convulsions (see Epilepsy): Diamond, Jasper, Chrysoprase

Cooling crystals: blue or pink stones, Lapis Lazuli, Larimar, Rose Quartz

Coordination, improve: Fluorite, Sugilite. *Chakra:* brow

Corns: Apatite (rub with, enhanced by soaking crystal in salt water)

Corpuscles, red: Chalcedony

Coughs: Amber, Ametrine, Aquamarine, Blue Agate, Topaz

Courage: Diamond, Topaz, Garnet. *Chakra:* heart

Cramp: Bloodstone, Amethyst, Malachite (use as polished stone, make remedy by indirect method), Magnesite, Obsidian, Serpentine, Smoky Quartz, Turquoise, Zircon, Magnetite (Lodestone)

>   **intestinal:** Green Fluorite, Magnesite
>   **legs:** Hematite, Lepidolite
>   **muscles:** Magnetite (Lodestone)

Unless otherwise directed, apply crystal over organ or site of symptom, place on appropriate chakra, wear as jewellery, bathe with or take as crystal remedy.

release: Azurite with Malachite (use as polished stone, make remedy by indirect method)

stomach: Magnesite

vascular: Magnesite

Cravings: Fire Agate. *Chakra:* solar plexus

Creativity, improve: Smoky Quartz, Spinel. *Chakra:* sacral.

Crown chakra: white and purple stones, see Chakras

Cruelty, overcome: Larimar. *Chakra:* heart

'Cure-all': Clear Calcite, Quartz (wear continuously)

Curses:

removing: Shattuckite, Tiger's Eye. *Chakra:* heart, solar plexus, brow

turn back: Black Tourmaline. *Chakra:* throat

Unless otherwise directed, apply crystal over organ or site of symptom, place on appropriate chakra, wear as jewellery, bathe with or take as crystal remedy.

- D -

Dark moods, ameliorate: Rutilated Quartz. *Chakra:* solar plexus, brow

Deafness: Amber, Onyx, Rhodonite, Tourmaline

Death/dying, assisting transition: Amethyst, Lilac Kunzite, Hyalite. (Place by bed or hold.) *Chakra:* higher crown

Decay, resist: Ruby (as a crystal remedy taken internally), Blue John, Pearl

Decision making, overcome inability in: Azurite, Rutilated Quartz, Green Tourmaline

Debility: Fire Agate, Black Tourmaline. *Chakra:* base

Degenerative:

   conditions of skin, hair, eyes, fleshy organs: Moonstone

   disease: Citrine, Brown Jasper

Dehydration: Moss Agate, Muscovite

Delirium: Peridot

Delusions, remove: Carnelian. *Chakra:* brow

Dementia: Chalcedony. *Chakra:* brow

Denial: Rhodochrosite. *Chakra:* heart

Unless otherwise directed, apply crystal over organ or site of symptom, place on appropriate chakra, wear as jewellery, bathe with or take as crystal remedy.

Dental:

    pain or problems: Fluorite

    plaque: Tarbuttite

Depression: <u>Lepidolite</u>, <u>Lithium Quartz</u>, <u>Kunzite</u>, <u>Ametrine</u>, <u>Sunstone</u>, Apatite, Botswana Agate, Carnelian, Idocrase, Jet, Lapis Lazuli, Moss Agate, Rutilated Quartz, Spessarite Garnet, Tiger's Eye, Hematite, Staurolite, Turquoise, Purple Tourmaline, Smoky Quartz, Siberian Quartz, Spinel, Jade. (Wear continuously.) *Chakra:* solar plexus

Depressive psychosis: Emerald (do not wear continuously, take as crystal remedy)

Deprivation, overcome: Rose Quartz, Prehnite (wear continuously). *Chakra:* higher heart

Dermatitis: Plume Agate (bathe in crystal remedy)

Despair: Rhodonite, Carnelian, Iron Pyrite, Serpentine, Sugilite (wear continuously). *Chakra:* heart

Despondency: Harlequin Quartz. *Chakra:* heart

Detoxification: brown or black stones, <u>Smoky Quartz</u>, Amethyst, Azurite, Bloodstone, Herkimer Diamond, Iolite, Obsidian (do not wear continuously), Stillbite, Ruby, Topaz, Zoisite. *Chakra:* solar plexus, earth, base

    emotions: Rose Quartz, Smoky Quartz. *Chakra:* solar plexus

    etheric: Lapis Lazuli. *Chakra:* brow

Unless otherwise directed, apply crystal over organ or site of symptom, place on appropriate chakra, wear as jewellery, bathe with or take as crystal remedy.

mind: Amethyst. *Chakra:* brow

physical body: Ruby. *Chakra:* earth, base, sacral

spiritual: Amethyst, Lapis Lazuli. *Chakra:* crown

Dexterity, improve: Chrysoprase

Diabetes: Citrine, Emerald, Red Jasper, Malachite (use as polished stone, make remedy by indirect method) Serpentine, Pink Opal, Jade, Diamond (worn at waist, on left side, as close to the pancreas as possible.)

Diagnosis, assist: Hiddenite, Blue Tourmaline

Diarrhoea: Green Tourmaline, Quartz, Malachite (use as polished stone, make remedy by indirect method), Serpentine, Pearl, Lapis Lazuli

loose green stools, especially in children: Sapphire

Digestion: Citrine, Chrysocolla, Labradorite, Smithsonite, Obsidian, Iron Pyrite, Sapphire, Snowflake Obsidian, Tiger's Eye, Topaz, Yellow Apatite, Topaz, Rhodonite, Peridot. *Chakra:* solar plexus

dis-ease due to stress: Moonstone

faulty: Red Tourmaline, Yellow Jasper

Digestive organs, strengthen: Jasper, Topaz. *Chakra:* solar plexus

Digestive tract: Amethyst, Chrysocolla, Pink Tourmaline

calm: Chrysoprase, Green Jasper, Chrysocolla, Iron Pyrite

stimulate: Red Jade, Moss Agate

Unless otherwise directed, apply crystal over organ or site of symptom, place on appropriate chakra, wear as jewellery, bathe with or take as crystal remedy.

strengthen: Iron Pyrite

Discs, loss of elasticity: Aragonite

Disease, infectious: Dioptase (tape over higher heart chakra)

Distress: Muscovite. *Chakra:* heart

Diuretic: Angelite (over kidneys)

Diverticulosis: Idocrase

Divine manifestation, increase trust in: Prehnite. *Chakra:* higher crown

Dizziness: Aragonite, Candle Quartz, Dioptase, Lapis Lazuli, Clear Quartz, White Sapphire. *Chakra:* crown

DNA: Beta Quartz, Ametrine, Fluorite, Garnet, Selenite, Phenacite, Azurite with Malachite and Chrysocolla (use as polished stone, make remedy by indirect method). *Chakra:* higher heart

 degeneration, reverse: Herkimer Diamond, Yellow Kunzite

 repair: Selenite, Phenacite, Fluorite, Garnet, Herkimer Diamond, Iron Pyrite, Lepidolite, Yellow Kunzite

Dropsy: Bloodstone, Amber, Jet. (Place over kidneys.)

Drunkenness: Amethyst, Tiger's Eye. (Wear continuously.)

Dry mouth: Candle Quartz

Duodenum: Peridot

Dysentery: Emerald, Chlorite

Dyslexia: Sugilite, Malachite (use as polished stone, make remedy by indirect method), Royal Sapphire, Tourmaline, Tourmalinated Quartz. *Chakra:* brow

Dyspepsia: Emerald

Dyspraxia: Muscovite. *Chakra:* brow

Unless otherwise directed, apply crystal over organ or site of symptom, place on appropriate chakra, wear as jewellery, bathe with or take as crystal remedy.

- E -

Ears: Amazonite, Amber, Blue Chalcedony, Celestite, Hiddenite, Red-black or Snowflake Obsidian, Orange Calcite, Rhodonite, Tourmaline (and see Hearing)

Ear problems: Amethyst, Blue Agate, Sapphire, Amber, Tourmaline

Earth healing: brown stones, Brown Aragonite, Smoky Quartz, Blue Sapphire, Prehnite, Brown Aragonite. *Chakra:* earth

    draw off negative energies: Smoky Quartz, Labradorite, Black Tourmaline, Black Obsidian

Eczema: Amethyst, Green Aventurine, Sapphire (bathe with alcohol-free crystal remedy)

Egotism: Magnesite. *Chakra:* base

Electromagnetic pollution: Smoky Quartz, Lepidolite, Amazonite, Jasper, Herkimer Diamond, Yellow Kunzite, Sodalite, Black Tourmaline. (Place stones on electrical equipment or around four corners of the house.) *Chakra:* earth

Elimination of waste products: Sardonyx. *Chakra:* base

Emotional: pink stones, Lapis Lazuli, Rose Quartz. *Chakra:* solar plexus, heart

---

abuse: Rose Quartz, Pink Carnelian, Pink Agate. *Chakra:* sacral, heart

baggage: pink or yellow stones, Petalite. *Chakra:* solar plexus

black hole: Dioptase. *Chakra:* higher heart

blackmail: Fuchsite. *Chakra:* solar plexus

blockages: yellow stones, Kunzite, Kyanite, Malachite (use as polished stone, make remedy by indirect method), Rose Quartz, Blue Tourmaline. *Chakra:* solar plexus

blockages from past lives: Lepidolite. *Chakra:* past life

bond in relationships, heal weak: Diamond. *Chakra:* heart

bondage: Lapis Lazuli crystal essence. *Chakra:* solar plexus

burn-out: Tiger Iron. *Chakra:* heart

conditioning: Rose Quartz. *Chakra:* solar plexus, brow

dependency: Lepidolite. *Chakra:* base

debris: Kunzite. *Chakra:* solar plexus

dysfunction: Watermelon Tourmaline. *Chakra:* higher heart

exhaustion: Apatite, Kunzite, Amethyst, Aragonite, Lepidolite, Azurite (especially when combined with Malachite), Magnesite, Orange Carnelian

hooks: Sunstone. *Chakra:* solar plexus

Unless otherwise directed, apply crystal over organ or site of symptom, place on appropriate chakra, wear as jewellery, bathe with or take as crystal remedy.

manipulation: Pink Carnelian. *Chakra:* sacral, solar plexus, brow

negative, destructive attachments: Chrysocolla. *Chakra:* base, solar plexus

pain: Pink or Watermelon Tourmaline. *Chakra:* higher heart

patterns: Moonstone. *Chakra:* solar plexus, base

recovery: Green Opal, Lapis Lazuli, Chrysocolla. *Chakra:* higher heart

release: Jade. *Chakra:* solar plexus, base, sacral

shock: Rhodonite. *Chakra:* heart

stability: Lepidolite, Rhodocrosite. *Chakra:* base

strength: Amethyst, Rose Quartz. *Chakra:* heart

stress: Kunzite. *Chakra:* solar plexus

tension: Fuchsite, Moonstone. *Chakra:* solar plexus

trauma: Amazonite, Amethyst, Aqua Aura, Rose Quartz *Chakra:* solar plexus

turmoil: Charoite. *Chakra:* base

wounds: Blue-green Smithsonite, Charoite, Rhodochrosite. *Chakra:* higher heart

underlying causes of distress: Ametrine. *Chakra:* solar plexus, past life

Emphysemia: Amber, Amethyst, Aqua Aura, Dioptase, Emerald, Malachite (use as polished stone, make remedy by indirect method), Morganite, Rhodonite, Rose Quartz,

Unless otherwise directed, apply crystal over organ or site of symptom, place on appropriate chakra, wear as jewellery, bathe with or take as crystal remedy.

Tiger's Eye

Empty nest syndrome: Zincite. *Chakra:* sacral

Endocrine system: Amber, Amethyst, Citrine, Fire Agate, Howlite, Pink Tourmaline, Golden Topaz, Yellow Jasper, Peridot, Pietersite, Tourmaline, Ruby Aura Quartz. *Chakra:* higher heart

Endometriosis: Vanadinite (make remedy by indirect method). *Chakra:* sacral

Endurance, promote: Jade. *Chakra:* base

Energy boost: red or orange stones, Amethyst, Carnelian, Herkimer Diamond. *Chakra:* base, sacral

Energy: red stones, <u>Jasper</u>, Quartz, Amber, Peridot. *Chakra:* base

> **depletion:** Fire Opal, Rutilated Quartz, Red or Yellow Jasper
>
> **field, strengthen:** Quartz, Kunzite. *Chakra:* solar plexus
>
> **implants:** Chlorite Phantom. *Chakra:* solar plexus, sacral
>
> **leakage from aura:** Labradorite. *Chakra:* higher heart
>
> **redistribution:** Garnet
>
> **unbalanced field:** Goldsheen Obsidian

Endurance: Chalcedony, Jade. *Chakra:* base, sacral

Entities, remove attached: Larimar, Fairy Quartz, Smoky Amethyst or Amethyst and Smoky Quartz. *Chakra:* sacral, solar plexus, brow

---

Unless otherwise directed, apply crystal over organ or site of symptom, place on appropriate chakra, wear as jewellery, bathe with or take as crystal remedy.

Environmental pollution: brown stones, Moss Agate, Smoky Quartz. (Place stones in earth or around house.) *Chakra:* earth

Envy, ameliorate: Ruby. *Chakra:* solar plexus, heart

Enzymes: Cupsidine

Epilepsy: Black Onyx (wear around the neck as prevention), Tourmaline, Emerald, Jasper, Jet, Lepidolite, Magnesite, Malachite (use as polished stone, make remedy by indirect method), Selenite, Sugilite, Tourmaline, Lapis Lazuli, Emerald, Yellow Sapphire. *Chakra:* brow

Eruptions: Galena (bathe with alcohol-free crystal remedy made by indirect method)

   on skin: Galena (make remedy by indirect method), Smithsonite

Etheric blueprint: Blue Opal (wear continuously or place on chakra). *Chakra:* past life

Eustation tubes, blocked: Celestite, Lapis Lazuli

Everyday reality, difficulty in dealing with: Smoky Quartz (wear continuously). *Chakra:* earth

Exhaustion: red or orange stones, <u>Carnelian</u>, Lepidolite, Ruby, Fire Opal, Pietersite, Rutilated Quartz, Sulphur (use as polished crystallized stone, make remedy by indirect method), Tiger's Eye, Turquoise. *Chakra:* sacral, base

Extremities, warm: Aragonite

Eyes: <u>Emerald</u> (bathe in alcohol-free crystal remedy), Cat's

Unless otherwise directed, apply crystal over organ or site of symptom, place on appropriate chakra, wear as jewellery, bathe with or take as crystal remedy.

Eye, Aquamarine, Agate, Beryl, Chalcedony, Sapphire, Charoite, Dark-blue Tourmaline, Blue Fluorite, Dendritic Agate, Ruby, Fire Agate, Snowflake Obsidian, Peridot, Opal, Blue Obsidian, Apophyllite, Iceland Spa, Labradorite, Celestite, Chrysoprase, Ulexite, Orange Calcite, Blue Lace Agate

> **bloodshot:** Emerald (bathe in alcohol-free crystal remedy)
>
> **clear:** Snowflake Obsidian
>
> **disease:** Jade, Albite
>
> **impurities, irritants in:** Ruby
>
> **infection:** Blue Lace Agate, Sapphire, Quartz, Ruby
>
> **itching:** Aquamarine
>
> **soothe:** Emerald
>
> **strengthen muscles:** Ulexite
>
> **tired:** Emerald
>
> **ulcerated:** Sapphire
>
> **watering:** Aqua Aura, Aquamarine
>
> **weak:** Pearl

Eyesight: green stones, Snowflake Obsidian, Rose Quartz, Malachite (use as polished stone, make remedy by indirect method), Variscite. *Chakra:* brow

> **weak:** Pyrolusite, Rhodochrosite, Opal

Unless otherwise directed, apply crystal over organ or site of symptom, place on appropriate chakra, wear as jewellery, bathe with or take as crystal remedy.

- F -

Facial pain: Cat's Eye, Cathedral Quartz

Facial paralysis: Diamond

Fainting: Amethyst, Lapis Lazuli

Fallopian tubes: Chrysoprase, Carnelian. *Chakra:* sacral

Family stress: Tiger Iron. *Chakra:* solar plexus

Fat metabolism, slow: Magnesite

Fatigue: Carnelian, Amethyst, Ametrine, Bloodstone, Blue Opal, Dendritic Agate, Iron Pyrite, Rose Quartz, Sunstone, Dioptase, Staurolite, Dioptase, Hematite. *Chakra:* base, sacral

Fatty deposits in body: Iolite

Fear: Rose Quartz, Rutilated Quartz (wear continuously), Emerald (take as crystal remedy). *Chakra:* heart, solar plexus

> **of failure:** Hematite
>
> **of responsibility:** Citrine

Feet: Tiger Iron, Onyx, Pietersite, Larimar, Smoky Quartz, Apophyllite, Aquamarine, Jet

> **burning:** Blue Lace Agate
>
> **excessive perspiration:** Gem Silica
>
> **swollen:** Aquamarine

Unless otherwise directed, apply crystal over organ or site of symptom, place on appropriate chakra, wear as jewellery, bathe with or take as crystal remedy.

Female reproductive system: orange stones, Carnelian, Malachite (use as polished stone, make remedy by indirect method), Moonstone, Chrysoprase, Amber, Topaz, Unakite, Wulfenite. *Chakra:* sacral, base

    inflammation: Dendritic Chalcedony

Feng shui: Prehnite

Fertility, increase: Atacamite, Carnelian, Jade, Moonstone, Orange Sapphire, Rose Quartz, Ruby in Zoisite. *Chakra:* sacral

Fever, lower: <u>Blue Chalcedony</u>, Agate, Chiastolite, Carnelian, Green Calcite, Hematite, Iolite, Iron Pyrite, Larimar, Kyanite, Okenite, Opal, Magnesite, Peridot, Moldavite, Tektite, Red Jasper, Peridot, Chlorite, Chrysoprase, Sapphire, Pearl (Place stone over site of greatest heat, place on brow or take as crystal remedy)

Fibroids: Vanadinite (make remedy by indirect method). *Chakra:* sacral

Fibrous growths: Sulphur (use as polished crystallized stone, make remedy by indirect method). *Chakra:* sacral

Finger nails, strengthen: Blue Lace Agate

'First aid': Rhodonite, Quartz

Flatulence: Green Garnet, Emerald, Diamond

Flexibility: Selenite, Azurite with Malachite (use as polished stone, make remedy by indirect method)

Flu: Fluorite, Labradorite, Moss Agate. *Chakra:* higher heart

Fluid:

> **deficiency:** Moonstone. *Chakra:* solar plexus
>
> **excess:** Rose Quartz, Jade, Diamond. *Chakra:* solar plexus
>
> **imbalances:** Jade, Moonstone. *Chakra:* solar plexus
>
> **retention:** Amber, Aquamarine, Aqua Aura, Jade, Moonstone. *Chakra:* solar plexus

Food poisoning: Emerald

Forgetfulness: Rhodonite, Emerald, Unakite, Tourmaline, Moss Agate. *Chakra:* brow

Forgiveness: Mangano Calcite (wear continuously), Chrysoberyl, Chrysoprase, Apache Tear, Rhodonite, Infinite Stone, Okenite, Rose Quartz, Rutilated Quartz, Sugilite. *Chakra:* higher heart

Fractures: Blue Lace Agate, Calcite, Hematite, Malachite (use as polished stone, make remedy by indirect method), Magnetite (Lodestone), Onyx, Tiger's Eye, Azurite with Malachite and Chrysocolla (use as polished stone, make remedy by indirect method)

Frailty: Chrysoprase. *Chakra:* higher heart

Free radical damage: Selenite. *Chakra:* higher heart

Fright: Opal, Lapis Lazuli. *Chakra:* solar plexus, heart

Frigidity: Carnelian, Uvarovite Garnet, Rose Quartz. *Chakra:* sacral, base

Frozen shoulder: Hawk's Eye

Unless otherwise directed, apply crystal over organ or site of symptom, place on appropriate chakra, wear as jewellery, bathe with or take as crystal remedy.

Frustration, overcome: Obsidian. *Chakra:* base

Fungal infection: <u>Moss Agate</u>, Chrysoprase with Smoky Quartz, Ruby Aura Quartz. (Bathe with crystal remedy or place stone over site)

Unless otherwise directed, apply crystal over organ or site of symptom, place on appropriate chakra, wear as jewellery, bathe with or take as crystal remedy.

- G -

Gallbladder: Amber, Yellow Apatite, Azurite with Malachite (use as polished stone, make remedy by indirect method), Calcite, Carnelian, Citrine, Chalcedony, Danburite, Green Obsidian, Peridot, Red Jasper, Tiger's Eye, Topaz

Gallstones: Carnelian, Rhyolite, Jasper, Emerald and Blue Sapphire

Garden health: Prehnite, Moss Agate (place around edges)

Gastric disturbance causing insomnia: Iron Pyrite. *Chakra:* solar plexus

Gastric:

    ulcer: Emerald, Sapphire, Agate. *Chakra:* solar plexus

    upset: Carnelian, Jasper, Thulite. *Chakra:* solar plexus

Gastritis: Agate

Genitals: Atacamite. *Chakra:* base

Geopathic stress: Amazonite, Amethyst, Brown Jasper, Kunzite, Smoky Quartz, Black Tourmaline, Selenite. (Place around corners of house.) *Chakra:* earth

Giddiness: Emerald, Quartz, Pearl

Gingivitis: Blue Lace Agate

Glands: Mookaite. *Chakra:* throat

regulate: Ruby

swollen: Aquamarine, Blue Lace Agate, Jet, Topaz

Glandular fever: Blue Lace Agate. *Chakra:* throat

Glandular swellings: Amber

Glaucoma: Blue Chalcedony, Diamond (bathe with alcohol-free crystal remedy)

Goitre: Amber (wear continuously), Chrysoprase, Zeolite. *Chakra:* throat

Gout: Chiastolite, Chrysoprase, Prehnite, Labradorite, Topaz, Tourmaline, Magnetite (Lodestone)

Greed, moderate: Opal. *Chakra:* base, solar plexus

Grief: Azurite, Red Jasper, Clear Obsidian, Lapis Lazuli, Rhodochrosite, Mangano Calcite. *Chakra:* higher heart

Grounding: brown stones, Herkimer Diamond, Boji Stone, Smoky Quartz, Hematite, Jasper, Black or Mahogany Obsidian. *Chakra:* base, earth

Growth, slow: Calcite

Growths: Malachite (use as polished stone, make remedy by indirect method)

Guilt: Chrysocolla, Peridot, Rose Quartz, Jasper, Larimar. *Chakra:* solar plexus, higher heart

Gums: Agate, Pyrolusite

- H -

Habits, overcome: Phenacite (wear continuously). *Chakra:* solar plexus

Haemophillia: Ruby

Haemorrhoids: Ametrine, Clear Obsidian, Ruby, Sapphire, Chrysocolla (bathe or add to bathwater), Golden Topaz, Bloodstone, Pearl

Haemorrhage: Bloodstone, Ruby, Topaz, Cat's Eye (Place over site.)

Hair: Aquamarine, Agate, Larimar, Galena (make remedy by indirect method), Opal, Tourmaline, Chrysocolla, Rutilated Quartz ('Angel Hair'). (Rinse with crystal remedy or wear stones as earrings.) *Chakra:* crown

    alopecia: Moonstone (massage scalp with stone, wear as earrings, or apply crystal remedy), Galena (make remedy by indirect method and use as a rinse). *Chakra:* solar plexus – brings up underlying cause

    baldness: Galena (make remedy by indirect method), Unakite (massage scalp)

    growth, stimulate: Galena (make remedy by indirect method), Chalcopyrite, Petrified Wood (massage with stone, or rinse with crystal remedy)

Unless otherwise directed, apply crystal over organ or site of symptom, place on appropriate chakra, wear as jewellery, bathe with or take as crystal remedy.

health: Jade (massage with stone, wear earrings, or rinse with crystal remedy)

loss: Galena (make remedy by indirect method), Aragonite (rinse with crystal remedy), Blue Opal (place on solar plexus, wear as earrings)

loss of condition: Chrysocolla, Quartz, Larimar, Magnetite (Lodestone), Opal, Smithsonite, Tourmaline, Unakite, Zincite (rinse in crystal remedy or wear stone as earrings) Galena (make remedy by indirect method and use as rinse)

pigmentation, lack of: Chrysocolla (use crystal remedy as a rinse or massage with stone)

problem: Magnetite (take as crystal remedy)

static electricity in: Unakite (rub through hair, wear as earrings, or rinse in crystal remedy)

Hallucinations: Lapis Lazuli. *Chakra:* brow, crown

Hands: Moldavite, Aquamarine, Moonstone, Smoky Quartz (Hold or wear crystal.)

swollen: Aquamarine, Moonstone

Hand–eye coordination: Tourmaline. *Chakra:* brow

Happiness: Sunstone (wear continuously). *Chakra:* heart

Hardened tissue: Rhyolite (massage with stone)

Harmony, promote: Rhodonite, Jade, Moonstone, Opal, Spinel, Picture Jasper. *Chakra:* solar plexus, heart

Hay fever: Amber, Aquamarine, Blue Lace Agate, Jet,

Tiger's Eye, Zircon (Wear continuously.)

Head: Larimar

> **excess energy in:** Brecciated Jasper

Headache: <u>Cathedral Quartz</u>, <u>Lapis Lazuli</u>, <u>Sugilite</u>, Amber, Amethyst, Dioptase, Magnesite, Smoky Quartz, Hematite, Rose Quartz, Turquoise, Jet, Blue Sapphire. *Chakra:* brow

> **arising from:**
>
>> **neck tension:** Magnetite (Lodestone) (on base of skull)
>>
>> **negative environmental factors/electromagnetic stress:** Smoky Quartz
>>
>> **poor posture:** Magnetite (Lodestone) (on base of skull)
>>
>> **upset stomach:** Ametrine (over stomach)

Healing crisis: Azurite crystal remedy taken every few minutes. *Chakra:* higher heart

Healing the healer: Prehnite. *Chakra:* higher heart

Hearing: Amethyst, Blue Agate, Rhodonite

> **disorders:** Amethyst
>
> **loss:** Lapis Lazuli

Heart: pink or green stones, <u>Rhodochrosite,</u> Green Obsidian, Peridot, Rose Quartz, Pink or Watermelon Tourmaline, Rhodonite, Blue or Green Aventurine, Sapphire. *Chakra:* heart

---

Unless otherwise directed, apply crystal over organ or site of symptom, place on appropriate chakra, wear as jewellery, bathe with or take as crystal remedy.

attacks: Aventurine, Dioptase

beat, irregular: Rhodochrosite, Jade

burn: Carnelian, Dioptase, Quartz, Peridot, Pyrope Garnet, Emerald

chakra: see Chakras

disease: Ruby, Red Jasper, Carnelian, Morganite, Rhodochrosite, Rhodonite, Tourmalinated Quartz

inflammation: Hematite

invigorate: Green Garnet

muscle: Kunzite

rhythm, disturbed: Serpentine

strengthen: Calcite

trauma: Larimar

unblock: Dioptase, Rose Quartz

Heartache: Chrysocolla, Lapis Lazuli, Rhodonite, Rose Quartz, Topaz, Lepidolite. (Wear continuously over the higher heart chakra.) *Chakra:* higher heart

Heatstroke: Blue Lace Agate, Hematite

Heavy metals, mobilize: Chrysoprase. *Chakra:* spleen

Helplessness: Golden Topaz, Smoky Quartz, Brown Tourmaline. *Chakra:* earth

Hepatitis: Calcite, Emerald

Hernia: Mookaite

Herpes: Fluorite, Jadeite, Lapis Lazuli. *Chakra:* throat

Hiatus hernia: Green Jasper (tape over site)

Unless otherwise directed, apply crystal over organ or site of symptom, place on appropriate chakra, wear as jewellery, bathe with or take as crystal remedy.

Hiccups: Peridot

Higher mind, calm and balance: Peridot. *Chakra:* brow

High blood pressure: see Blood pressure

Hips: Jade, Tiger Iron, Smoky Quartz, Red Calcite
   pain: Azurite

Hoarseness: Sodalite. *Chakra:* throat

'Hooks' from others, removing: Sunstone, Fairy Quartz, Smoky Amethyst. *Chakra:* sacral, solar plexus, brow

Hormones:
   boosting: Amethyst, Pietersite. *Chakra:* brow, higher heart
   for growth: Pietersite. *Chakra:* brow, higher heart
   imbalances: Chrysoprase, Citrine, Labradorite, Moonstone. *Chakra:* brow, higher heart
   regulate: Watermelon Tourmaline. *Chakra:* brow, higher heart

Hospitalization: Jasper

Hostility, overcome: Sugilite (wear continuously). *Chakra:* higher heart, base

Hot flushes: Fire Agate, Citrine

Hunger pangs: Muscovite

Hydrocephalus: Blue Lace Agate

Hyperacidity: Emerald

Hyperactivy: Cerussite, Garnet, Green Tourmaline, Moonstone, Ruby. *Chakra:* earth, base

---

Unless otherwise directed, apply crystal over organ or site of symptom, place on appropriate chakra, wear as jewellery, bathe with or take as crystal remedy.

Hypertension: Apatite

Hyperthyroidism: Atacamite. *Chakra:* throat

Hypochondria: Tiger's Eye, Blue Agate, Peridot. *Chakra:* solar plexus

Hypoglycemia: Moss Agate, Serpentine, Pink Opal. *Chakra:* spleen

Hysterectomy: Chrysocolla

Hysteria: Lapis Lazuli, Rose Quartz, Amber, Turquoise, Amethyst, Topaz, Moonstone (use with caution, remove if worse). *Chakra:* solar plexus

- I -

Incest, overcome effects: Rhodonite, Rhodochrosite, Lapis Lazuli. (Wear continuously, or place over chakras for 20 minutes daily). *Chakra:* base, sacral, solar plexus

'Identified patient' (the person who takes on the family pain or dis-ease and who becomes ill, or addicted, on behalf of the family, as it were, so that other members can remain healthy): Fuchsite

Idleness, overcome: Morganite, Aquamarine, Emerald, Garnet. *Chakra:* base

Ill-wishing: Black Tourmaline (wear continuously). *Chakra:* throat

Immune system: <u>Bloodstone</u> (wear continuously over higher heart chakra), <u>Smithsonite</u> (place around corners of bed), Chevron Amethyst, Ametrine, Black or Green Tourmaline, Brown Jasper, Green Calcite, Chiastolite, Lepidolite, Mookaite, Kunzite, Lapis Lazuli, Blue Agate, Carnelian, Malachite (use as polished stone, make remedy by indirect method), Moss Agate, Quartz, Ruby in Zoisite, Turquoise. *Chakra:* higher heart

Impacted vertebrae: Electric-blue Obsidian, Labradorite

Implants: Petalite. *Chakra:* crown

Unless otherwise directed, apply crystal over organ or site of symptom, place on appropriate chakra, wear as jewellery, bathe with or take as crystal remedy.

Impotence: Carnelian, Garnet, Morganite, Rhodonite, Sodalite, Variscite. *Chakra:* base, sacral

Incontinence: Petrified Wood. *Chakra:* sacral

Indigestion: Candle Quartz, Citrine, Jasper, Peridot, Tourmaline. *Chakra:* solar plexus

Indulgence, overcome effects of: Amethyst, Bloodstone (wear continuously)

Inertia: red stones, Iron Pyrite, Zircon. *Chakra:* base, sacral

Infection: Blue Lace Agate, Kunzite, Galena (make remedy by indirect method), Green Calcite, Opal, Amethyst, Smoky Quartz, Sulphur (spray room with crystal remedy made by indirect method). *Chakra:* higher heart

> **acute:** Bloodstone, Chrysocolla, Rhodochrosite, Sulphur (use as polished crystallized stone, make remedy by indirect method)

> **increase resistance to:** Amethyst (wear continuously)

Infectious illness: Emerald, Fluorite. *Chakra:* higher heart

Infertility: Moonstone, Thulite, Zincite, Garnet. *Chakra:* sacral

> **arising from infection:** Chrysoprase

Inflammation: Blue Lace Agate, Blue Chalcedony, Galena (make remedy by indirect method), Green Jasper, Larimar, Iron Pyrites, Siberian Blue Quartz, Topaz, Spinel

> **bladder and intestinal:** Agate
> **kidneys:** Jade, Jadeite

Unless otherwise directed, apply crystal over organ or site of symptom, place on appropriate chakra, wear as jewellery, bathe with or take as crystal remedy.

joints: Rhodonite, Malachite (use as polished stone, make remedy by indirect method)

Influenza: Fluorite, Moss Agate. *Chakra:* higher heart

Inhibitions: Malachite (use as polished stone, make remedy by indirect method). *Chakra:* base

Injuries: Amethyst, Obsidian

Inner child: Amethyst. *Chakra:* sacral

Insect bites: Rhodonite

Insecurity: Muscovite. *Chakra:* base

Insomnia: <u>Ajoite</u>, Amethyst, Ajoite with Shattuckite, Candle Quartz, Celestite, Charoite, Hematite, Howlite, Lapis Lazuli, Lepidolite, Moonstone, Muscovite, Sodalite, Topaz, Zoisite, Magnetite (Lodestone). (Place at head and foot of bed.)

> **from geopathic/electromagnetic stress:** <u>Herkimer Diamond</u>, <u>Black Tourmaline</u>, Smoky Quartz. (Place round bed or around the four corners of the room or house, depending on how strong the stress)
>
> **from negative environmental influences:** Bloodstone in water by bed, Black Tourmaline placed around the four corners of the room
>
> **from nightmares:** Tourmaline, Smoky Quartz *Chakra:* brow
>
> **from overactive mind:** Blue Selenite, Yellow Labradorite, Amethyst *Chakra:* brow

---

Unless otherwise directed, apply crystal over organ or site of symptom, place on appropriate chakra, wear as jewellery, bathe with or take as crystal remedy.

from overeating: Iron Pyrite, Moonstone *Chakra:* solar plexus

from stress: Chrysoprase, Rose Quartz, Amethyst. *Chakra:* higher heart

Insults, turn away: Rhodonite. *Chakra:* higher heart

Insulin regulation: Chrysocolla, Opal, *Chakra:* spleen

Intellect:

    improve: Sapphire. *Chakra:* brow, crown

    stabilize: Cymophane. *Chakra:* brow, crown

Intestinal disorders: Orange Calcite, Brown Tourmaline. *Chakra:* sacral

Intestines: Amber, Amethyst, Beryl, Bloodstone, Carnelian, Calcite, Celestite, Green Fluorite, Fire Opal, Yellow Jasper, Petalite, Peridot, Snowflake Obsidian, Sardonyx, Apophyllite. *Chakra:* sacral

Introspection: Tree Agate. *Chakra:* brow

Involuntary movement: Celestite

Iron, malabsorption: Almandine Garnet, Hematite, Dioptase. *Chakra:* base

    improve assimilation: Chrysocolla

Irritable bowel syndrome: Calcite

Irritability: Apatite, Rhodonite, Jade. *Chakra:* base, sacral

Irritant filter: Rhodochrosite

Irritation: Peridot

Intuitive vision: Chevron Amethyst, Lapis Lazuli, Petalite,

Selenite, Labradorite, Sodalite, Phenacite. *Chakra:* brow, crown

Itching: Azurite, Malachite (use as polished stone, make remedy by indirect method), Green Aventurine, Hematite

Unless otherwise directed, apply crystal over organ or site of symptom, place on appropriate chakra, wear as jewellery, bathe with or take as crystal remedy.

- J -

Jaw: Aquamarine

Jaundice: Ametrine, Jadeite, Yellow Sapphire

Jealousy: Amethyst, Peridot, Apophyllite, Rhodochrosite, Chrysanthemum Stone. *Chakra:* heart

Jet lag: Cerussite, Black Tourmaline (sip crystal remedy frequently)

Joints: <u>Magnetite (Lodestone)</u>, Hematite, Dioptase, Calcite, Azurite, Rhodonite

    calcified: Calcite

    inflammation: Hematite, Malachite (use as polished stone, make remedy by indirect method), Rhodonite, Hematite with Malachite (use as polished stone, make remedy by indirect method), Lapis Lazuli

    mobilizing: Fluorite, Red Calcite

    pain: Kunzite

    problems: Amber, Apatite, Fluorite, Lepidolite, Obsidian, Sulphur (use as polished crystallized stone, make remedy by indirect method)

    strengthening: Aragonite, Calcite

    swollen: Malachite (use as polished stone, make remedy by indirect method)

Unless otherwise directed, apply crystal over organ or site of symptom, place on appropriate chakra, wear as jewellery, bathe with or take as crystal remedy.

- K -

Karmic dis-ease: see Past Lives. *Chakra:* past life
Kennel cough: Amber, Hematite, Jadeite
Kidney: <u>Jade</u>, <u>Jadeite</u>, Amber, Aquamarine, Beryl, Bloodstone, Hematite, Carnelian, Chrysocolla, Muscovite, Septarian, Citrine, Orange Calcite, Nephrite, Rhodochrosite, Rose or Smoky Quartz, Serpentine, Topaz. *Chakra:* solar plexus

> **cleanser:** <u>Jade</u>, Atacamite, Nephrite, Hematite, Bloodstone, Opal, Rose Quartz
> **degeneration:** Honey Calcite, Red or Yellow Jasper
> **detoxify:** Chrysocolla, Smoky Quartz
> **fortify:** Grossularite
> **infections:** Citrine
> **regulating:** Carnelian, Muscovite
> **stimulating:** Ruby, Rhodochrosite
> **stones:** Magnesite, Rhyolite, Jasper
> **underactive:** Ruby, Fire Opal, Prehnite, Rhodochrosite
> **Knees:** Azurite, Blue Lace Agate

- L -

Lactation:
    impaired: Chalcedony, Okenite, Moonstone
    improve: Jade

Lactose intolerance: Spessarite Garnet

Labour pains: Lapis Lazuli (tape over site of pain)

Larynx: Blue Kyanite, Blue Tourmaline, Lapis Lazuli. *Chakra:* throat

Laryngitis: Amber, Blue Lace Agate, Rhodonite, Sodalite, Stillbite, Tourmaline. (Wear continuously over site or gargle with crystal remedy.) *Chakra:* throat

Learning difficulties: Sugilite (wear continuously). *Chakra:* brow, crown

Left–right confusion: Muscovite. *Chakra:* brow, crown

Legs: <u>Aquamarine</u>, Bloodstone, Blue Tiger's Eye, Garnet, Jasper, Pietersite, Hawk's Eye, Ruby, Smoky Quartz, Tiger Iron, Red Calcite

Leprosy: Ruby

Lethargy: Ametrine, Carnelian, Red Tiger's Eye, Ruby, Tourmaline. *Chakra:* base, sacral

Letting go past: Fire Opal. *Chakra:* solar plexus, heart, past life

---

Unless otherwise directed, apply crystal over organ or site of symptom, place on appropriate chakra, wear as jewellery, bathe with or take as crystal remedy.

Letting off steam constructively: Jade. *Chakra:* base

Leucorrhaea: Turquoise

Leukaemia: Bloodstone, Uvarovite Garnet, Alexandrite

Life force, increase: Aquamarine (wear continuously). *Chakra:* higher heart

Ligaments, torn: Staurolite, Stillbite

Light body: Kyanite, Petalite. *Chakra:* higher crown

Lightheadedness: Amethyst

Light sensitivity: Selenite

Liver: <u>Yellow Jasper</u>, Amethyst, Aquamarine, Azurite with Malachite (use as polished stone, make remedy by indirect method), Beryl, Bloodstone, Carnelian, Charoite, Citrine, Danburite, Emerald, Gold Calcite, Hiddenite, Labradorite, Rhodonite, Amber, Chrysoprase, Red Jasper, Yellow Fluorite, Yellow Labradorite, Pietersite, Rose Quartz, Ruby, Tiger's Eye, Topaz

    blockages: Red Jasper, Red Tourmaline

    cleanse: Ruby

    damage due to alcohol: Charoite, Peridot

    detoxifying: Malachite (use as polished stone, make remedy by indirect method)

    spots: Chlorite, Seraphinite

    stimulate: Azurite, Ziron, Emerald

Longevity: Agate, Chrysoberyl, Chrysoprase, Jade, Peridot, Sodalite, Rhodonite, Serpentine, Diamond

---

Lower-back problems: Carnelian, Fire Opal, Cathedral Quartz

Love: pink stones, <u>Rose Quartz</u>, <u>Sugilite</u>, <u>Rhodochrosite</u>, <u>Garnet</u>. *Chakra:* heart, higher heart

 accepting: Agate, Mangano Calcite, Rose Quartz

 and spirituality: Pink Tourmaline

 attract: Rose Quartz (place large chunk by bed), Rhodonite, Morganite (Wear continuously.)

 bond: Lapis Lazuli, Diamond

 bring in: Celestite

 combine logic with: Thulite

 desperate for: Dioptase

 fidelity: Diamond, Garnet

 for oneself: Magnesite

 foster: Agate

 increase capacity to: Chrysocolla

 mature: Green Aventurine

 of:

  divine: Amethyst, Petalite. *Chakra:* brow, crown

  self: Rose Quartz, Sugilite

  truthfulness: Agate

 old, cut the cords of: Rainbow Obsidian, Rainbow Quartz. *Chakra:* solar plexus, sacral, past life

 open to possibility of: Almandine Garnet

 parent–child: Pink Agate

promotion of: Rhodochrosite, Pink Sapphire, Diamond, Rhodonite

reawaken: Beryl

selfless: Rose Quartz, Rhodochrosite

tough love: Fuchsite

transform psychic attack into: Amethyst. *Chakra:* higher heart

unconditional: Atacamite, Emerald, Kunzite, Morganite, Magnesite, Cymophane, Mangano Calcite, Charoite. *Chakra:* higher heart

universal: Amazonite, Apophyllite

Lumbago: Candle Quartz, Magnetite (Lodestone), Sapphire (Wear continuously over site.)

Lungs: <u>Charoite</u>, Amber, Amethyst, Aventurine, Beryl, Fluorite, Chrysocolla, Dioptase, Hiddenite, Kunzite, Lapis Lazuli, Peridot, Petalite, Pink Tourmaline, Prehnite, Rose Quartz, Sodalite, Turquoise, Rhodochrosite, Sardonyx, Emerald, Morganite, Watermelon Tourmaline, Serpentine

congested: Vanadinite (make remedy by indirect method), Moss Agate

difficulty in breathing: Chrysocolla, Apophyllite (see also Breathlessness)

fluid in: Zircon, Amber, Diamond, Yellow Sapphire

Lust, excess: Onyx. *Chakra:* base, sacral

Lymphatic system: Agate, Moss Agate, Blue Chalcedony,

Tourmaline

cleansing: Yellow Apatite, Agate, Rose Quartz, Ruby, Light-coloured Sugilite, Sodalite

infections: Blue Lace Agate

stimulating: Bloodstone, Blue Chalcedony

swellings: Jet

- M -

Madness, fear of: Chiastolite. *Chakra:* brow

Magnesium absorption: Magnesite. *Chakra:* solar plexus

Malaria: Blue Lace Agate, Iolite, Turquoise

Male–female imbalance: Moonstone, Merlinite, Hematite with Rutile. *Chakra:* sacral

Malignant conditions: Emerald, Prehnite, Azurite, Alexandrite, Malachite (use as polished stone, make remedy by indirect method), Smoky Quartz, Amethyst, Magnetite (Lodestone), Carnelian, Garnet

Mania: Pearl

Martyrdom: Larimar, Lapis Lazuli. *Chakra:* higher heart, solar plexus

Mastectomy: Chrysocolla

Maternal instinct: Chalcedony. *Chakra:* base, sacral

ME: Ametrine, Ruby, Tourmaline (Wear continuously.)

Measles: Turquoise, Leopardskin Jasper, Topaz, Pearl

Melancholy: Lapis Lazuli, Sardonyx, Tourmaline, Sapphire. (Wear continuously.) *Chakra:* solar plexus

Meditative states, enter easily: Larimar, Apophyllite, Selenite, Yellow Labradorite, Amethyst. *Chakra:* brow, crown

Memory, improve: Amber, Amethyst, Opal, Rhodonite, Unakite, Emerald, Moss Agate, Pyrolusite. *Chakra:* brow, crown

Ménières disease: Dioptase (tape behind affected ear)

Menopause: Citrine, Garnet, Lapis Lazuli, Lepidolite, Cherry Opal, Pearl, Moonstone, Rose Quartz, Ruby, Zincite, Diamond, Ruby

Mental:

    breakdown: Rhodochrosite, Topaz. *Chakra:* brow, crown

    conditioning, rigid: Sodalite. *Chakra:* brow, crown

    dexterity, improve: Chrysoprase. *Chakra:* brow, crown

Menstruation:

    bring on: Wulfenite, Red Jasper. *Chakra:* sacral, base

    excessive: Carnelian, Jasper. *Chakra:* sacral, base

    irregular: Red Jasper. *Chakra:* sacral, base

Menstrual:

    cramps: Chrysocolla, Citrine, Infinite Stone, Jet, Labradorite, Lapis Lazuli, Magnesite, Rose Quartz, Topaz, Pearl. *Chakra:* sacral, base

    cycle, regulate: Carnelian, Moonstone. *Chakra:* sacral, base

    disorders: Staurolite, Topaz, Jet. *Chakra:* sacral, base

Mental:

    breakdown: Smithsonite. *Chakra:* brow, crown

burdens, lighten: Amethyst. *Chakra:* brow, crown

burn-out: Tiger Iron. *Chakra:* brow, crown

dependency: Lepidolite. *Chakra:* brow, crown

dis-ease: Tiger's Eye. *Chakra:* brow, crown

dysfunction: Celestite. *Chakra:* brow, crown

undue influence, remove: Fluorite, Sunstone. *Chakra:* brow, crown

Mercury toxicity: Rutilated Quartz, Smoky Quartz. *Chakra:* spleen

Meridians:

blocked: Larimar

harmonize: Tourmalinated Quartz

re-align: Muscovite

stimulate: Quartz

Metabolism, stimulate: Amethyst, Sodalite, Pyrolusite. *Chakra:* higher heart

Metabolic:

imbalances: Amazonite, Blue Opal, Diamond, Sodalite, Herkimer Diamond, Labradorite, Peridot, Watermelon Tourmaline, Azurite with Malachite and Chrysocolla (use as polished stone, make remedy by indirect method) *Chakra:* brow

stimulating processes: Apatite, Red Carnelian, Blue Tiger's Eye, Garnet *Chakra:* brow

system: Amethyst, Sodalite, Carnelian, Bloodstone,

Labradorite

Miasms: Azurite, Chrysocolla, Petalite, Sugilite, Rhodochrosite, Jet, Lapis Lazuli, Magnesite. *Chakra:* earth, base, past life

Mid-life crisis: Rose Quartz

Migraine: Aventurine, Dioptase, Iolite, Sugilite, Rhodochrosite, Jet, Lapis Lazuli, Magnesite, Rose Quartz, Topaz, Pearl. *Chakra:* brow, crown, past life

Mind: Magnesite 'brain form', Zircon. *Chakra:* brow, crown

> **focusing:** Amethyst, Fluorite, Idocrase
>
> **mind chatter, shut off:** Rhomboid Calcite, Blue Selenite (see also Over-thinking)
>
> **negative thought patterns:** Idocrase

Minerals:

> **balance in body:** Jasper (tape over solar plexus)
>
> **build-up in body:** Chalcedony (tape over kidneys)
>
> **non-assimilation:** Garnet, Smoky Quartz (tape over solar plexus)

Misfit: Sugilite. *Chakra:* base

Miscarriage, healing after: Wulfenite. *Chakra:* sacral

Mood swings: Turquoise (wear continuously). *Chakra:* solar plexus

Motion sickness: Linarite

Motor dysfunction: Danburite, Kyanite, Sugilite

Unless otherwise directed, apply crystal over organ or site of symptom, place on appropriate chakra, wear as jewellery, bathe with or take as crystal remedy.

Mouth: Apatite, Sodalite, Tiger's Eye, Yellow Sapphire

> **movement disorders:** Apophyllite, Albite
>
> **problems:** Beryl
>
> **ulcers:** Clear Quartz, Jadeite, Lapis Lazuli, Rose Quartz, Ruby, Tourmaline

Mucus membranes: Amber

Multiple sclerosis: Carnelian, Red Jasper, Rose Quartz, Lapis Lazuli, Rhodonite, Tourmaline, Blue John

Multiple personality disorder: Blue Obsidian

Mumps: Aquamarine, Topaz

Muscles: Hematite, Rhodonite, Jadeite

> **cramps:** <u>Magnetite (Lodestone)</u>, Apache Tear, Infinite Stone
>
> **flexibility:** Fuchsite, Petalite
>
> **relaxant:** Celestite, Larimar, Magnesite, Smithsonite
>
> **spasm:** <u>Azurite with Malachite</u> (use as polished stone, make remedy by indirect method), Amazonite, Apache Tear, Red Tourmaline, Chrysocolla, Magnetite (Lodestone)
>
> **strengthen:** Apatite, Fluorite, Tourmaline, Peridot, Jadeite
>
> **tissue:** Aventurine, Danburite, Magnetite (Lodestone)
>
> **tone:** Fluorite, Peridot, Tourmaline
>
> **torn:** Malachite (use as polished stone, make remedy by indirect method)

Unless otherwise directed, apply crystal over organ or site of symptom, place on appropriate chakra, wear as jewellery, bathe with or take as crystal remedy.

weak: Tiger Iron, Rhyolite

Muscular disorders: Kyanite, Peridot, Petalite

Muscular-skeletal system inflexibility: Fuchsite, Jade

- N -

Nails: Rhodochrosite, Blue Lace Agate

    strengthen: Calcite, Fluorite, Rhodochrosite, Pearl

Narrow-mindedness: Chrysanthemum Stone. *Chakra:* base, higher heart

Nasal passages: Larimar

Nausea: Red Aventurine, Dioptase, Emerald, Brown Agate, Fuchsite, Jasper, Blue Sapphire. *Chakra:* solar plexus

Navel/sacral chakra: orange stones, see Chakras

Neck: Aquamarine, Quartz, Larimar. *Chakra:* throat

    tension: Hematite, Magnetite (Lodestone), Rose Quartz, Seraphinite, Alexandrite

Negative:

    energy, dispel: Amber, Amethyst, Lapis Lazuli, Snowflake Obsidian, Smoky Quartz. *Chakra:* throat, earth

    ions, increase: Lepidolite

    karma: Petalite. *Chakra:* past life

    thoughts, dispel: Chiastolite, Lapis Lazuli. *Chakra:* brow

Negativity, dispel: Topaz, Carnelian. *Chakra:* earth

Nephritis: Tourmaline, Jade

Unless otherwise directed, apply crystal over organ or site of symptom, place on appropriate chakra, wear as jewellery, bathe with or take as crystal remedy.

Nerve damage: Fishtail Selenite, Chiastolite, Kunzite

Nerves: Dendritic Agate, Pink Tourmaline, Smoky Quartz, Amethyst

    calming: Amazonite

    pain relief: Fluorite

    regenerating: Watermelon Tourmaline

    strengthen: Jade

Nervous:

    autonomic system: Ametrine, Charoite, Sunstone

    disorders: Sapphire, Kunzite, Chrysoprase

    exhaustion: Thulite, Morganite

    stress: Muscovite

    system: Blue Lace Agate, Green Jade, Lapis Lazuli, Amber, Green Tourmaline

    tension: Emerald

Nervousness: Rhodochrosite, Lapis Lazuli, Sapphire (Wear continuously, or place for 20 minutes.)

Neuralgia: <u>Cathedral Quartz</u> (over site of pain), Amber, Amethyst, Carnelian, Dendritic Agate, Kunzite, Lapis Lazuli, Lepidolite, Hematite, Rose Quartz, Magnetite (Lodestone)

Neuritis: Tourmaline

Neurological tissue: Dendritic Agate

Neuroses: Aventurine (especially Green). *Chakra:* solar plexus

---

Unless otherwise directed, apply crystal over organ or site of symptom, place on appropriate chakra, wear as jewellery, bathe with or take as crystal remedy.

Neurotic patterns: Chrysoprase, Sapphire. *Chakra:* solar plexus

Nervous tics: Green Aventurine

Nightmares: Amethyst, Celestite, Chrysoprase, Mangano Calcite, Prehnite, Ruby, Turquoise, Smoky Quartz, Hematite, Jet. (Wear or keep under pillow.)

Night:

> **blindness:** Amethyst
>
> **cramps:** Magnetite (Lodestone)
>
> **sweats:** Blue Tourmaline
>
> **terrors:** Mangano Calcite, Prehnite, Spessarite, Topaz. (Wear or keep under pillow.) (Avoid Onyx)
>
> **twitches:** Aragonite (under pillow)
>
> **vision:** Cat's Eye, Tiger's Eye, Brown Jasper, Blue-green Obsidian

Nose bleeds: <u>Carnelian</u>, Magnetite (Lodestone), Topaz (apply externally to nostril), Sapphire (apply to forehead), Ruby

Nose problems: Blue Fluorite, Magnetite (Lodestone)

Nostrils, blocked: Jet (place over, or inhale essence)

Nuclear sites, neutralize radiation effects: Malachite (use as polished stone, make remedy by indirect method), Smoky Quartz. (Place stones around site.)

Nutrient malabsorption: Idocrase, Fluorite, Turquoise, Moonstone, Pietersite, Serpentine. *Chakra:* solar plexus

Nurturing, lack of: Selenite, Jade. *Chakra:* higher heart, base

---

Unless otherwise directed, apply crystal over organ or site of symptom, place on appropriate chakra, wear as jewellery, bathe with or take as crystal remedy.

- O -

Obesity: Black Onyx, Diamond, Tourmaline, Moonstone, Zircon

Obsession: Blue Agate, Black Onyx, Green Jasper, Peridot, Bloodstone, Charoite. *Chakra:* solar plexus, brow

Obsessive thoughts: Lepidolite, Purple Tourmaline. *Chakra:* brow, crown

Odour absorption: Zeolite

Oedema: Carnelian

Old age, overcome weakness in: Diamond

Optic nerve: Malachite (use as polished stone, make remedy by indirect method) *Chakra:* brow

Oesophagus: Blue Tourmaline. *Chakra:* throat

Olfactory system: Galena (make remedy by indirect method)

Osteoporosis: Amazonite, Larimar, Smithsonite

Otosclerosis: Ruby

Outworn patterns: Malachite (use as polished stone, make remedy by indirect method) *Chakra:* earth, base, sacral, solar plexus, brow

Ovaries: Amber, Atacamite, Carnelian, Chrysoprase, Gold Calcite, Peach Aventurine, Ruby in Zoisite, Topaz. *Chakra:*

Unless otherwise directed, apply crystal over organ or site of symptom, place on appropriate chakra, wear as jewellery, bathe with or take as crystal remedy.

sacral

    disease of: Zoisite

Over:

    acidification: Bloodstone, Chiastolite, Zoisite

    active: Amethyst, Garnet

    attachment: Magnetite (Lodestone). *Chakra:* solar plexus

    eating: Hematite. *Chakra:* base

    indulgence: Amethyst, Hematite. *Chakra:* base

    sensitive: Rose Quartz, Sodalite. *Chakra:* solar plexus

    thinking: Rhomboid Calcite, Yellow Labradorite, Beryl, Blue Selenite. *Chakra:* brow

    weight: Cinnabar

    whelm: Blue-green Jade (wear continuously). *Chakra:* solar plexus

    working: Staurolite

Oxygen, malabsorption: Serpentine (over heart and lungs)

- P -

Pain relief: <u>Cathedral Quartz</u>, Amber, Amethyst, Dendritic Agate, Boji Stones, Aragonite, Celestite, Fluorite, Hematite, Infinite Stone, Lapis Lazuli, Larimar, Malachite (use as polished stone, make remedy by indirect method), Magnetite (Lodestone), Quartz, Sugilite, Mahogany Obsidian, Seraphinite, Smoky Quartz, Rose Quartz, Tourmaline

Painful feelings, assimilate: Rhodochrosite. *Chakra:* solar plexus, higher heart

Palpitations: Garnet (wear continuously). *Chakra:* heart

Pancreas: Amber, Bloodstone, Charoite, Chrysocolla, Citrine, Carnelian, Green Calcite, Jasper, Malachite (use as polished stone, make remedy by indirect method), Moonstone, Pink Tourmaline, Smoky Quartz, Topaz, Red Tourmaline, Blue Lace Agate, Chrysocolla, Septarian. *Chakra:* spleen

Pancreatic secretions: Muscovite, Malachite (use as polished stone, make remedy by indirect method) *Chakra:* spleen, solar plexus, base

Panic attacks: <u>Kunzite</u>, Blue-green Smithsonite, Turquoise, Green Tourmaline. (Keep in pocket and hold when required.) *Chakra:* heart, solar plexus

Paralysis: Amethyst, Chiastolite, Watermelon Tourmaline, Emerald with Blue Sapphire. (Place stones in bath or take as crystal remedy.)

Paranoia: Rhodochrosite, Sugilite. *Chakra:* base, solar plexus

Parasites: Amethyst, Ruby Aura Quartz, Rutilated Quartz, Serpentine. (Take as crystal remedy and place over site of infestation.)

Parathyroid: Kyanite, Malachite (use as polished stone, make remedy by indirect method) *Chakra:* throat

Parkinsons disease: Celestite, Opal, Rose Quartz

Past, release from: Mangano Calcite. *Chakra:* past life, earth, base

Past life:

> **abandonment:** Rhodonite, Pink Tourmaline. *Chakra:* past life, heart
>
> **access:** Variscite, Wulfenite. *Chakra:* past life, brow
>
> **addiction, causes of:** Iolite. *Chakra:* past life, base
>
> **akashic record, read:** Tibetan Black Spot Quartz, Cathedral Quartz, Tanzanite, Prehnite. *Chakra:* past life, brow, crown
>
> **betrayal:** Rhodonite. *Chakra:* past life, heart
>
> **blockages from past lives:** Lepidolite. *Chakra:* past life
>
> **broken heart:** Rose Quartz. *Chakra:* past life, heart

chastity: Okenite. *Chakra*: past life, base, sacral

cleansing: Danburite. *Chakra:* past life

curses:

> **break:** Shattuckite, Tiger's Eye. *Chakra:* past life, throat, brow
>
> **deflect effects of:** Black Tourmaline. *Chakra:* past life, throat

cycles: Okenite. *Chakra:* past life

death, unhealed trauma: Lilac Smithsonite. *Chakra:* past life, earth, base, heart

debts, recognize: Okenite. *Chakra:* past life, solar plexus

deprivation: Prehnite. *Chakra:* past life, base, higher heart

dis-ease: Tanzanite with Iolite and Danburite. *Chakra:* past life

emotional:

> **attachments:** Rainbow Aura Quartz, Rainbow Obsidian. (Wear continuously.) *Chakra:* past life
>
> **pain:** Charoite. *Chakra:* past life, heart, higher heart, solar plexus
>
> **wounds:** Rhodonite. *Chakra:* past life, heart, higher heart, solar plexus

entity attachment: Smoky Amethyst, Kunzite, Larimar, Petalite, Selenite, Laser Quartz. (Place on appropriate chakra, hold in place until removed, purify crystal immediately.) *Chakra:* past life, sacral, solar plexus, brow

family patterns: Spirit Quartz. *Chakra:* past life, sacral

grief, unhealed: Fire Opal, Spirit Quartz. *Chakra:* past life, heart

hyperactivity due to effects of: Prehnite. *Chakra:* past life, brow

healing: Danburite, Merlinite, Charoite, Obsidian, Okenite, Infinite Stone, Rhodonite, Pietersite. *Chakra:* past life

heart pain: Rhodonite, Rhodochrosite, Dioptase. *Chakra:* past life, higher heart

injuries: Herkimer Diamond, Onyx. *Chakra:* past life

learning from: Muscovite, Peridot. *Chakra:* past life

mental imperatives, release: Danburite, Idocrase. *Chakra:* past life

persecution: Wulfenite. *Chakra:* past life

phobias resulting from: Prehnite. *Chakra:* past life

prisoner: Idocrase. *Chakra:* past life, base

psychosexual problems resulting from: Malachite (use as polished stone, make remedy by indirect method). *Chakra:* past life, base, sacral

recall: Amber, Carnelian, Phantom Crystals, Garnet, Serpentine, Variscite. *Chakra:* past life, brow

redress: Charoite. *Chakra:* past life

regression: Green Aventurine, Variscite. *Chakra:* past life, brow

relationships: Larimar, Lithium Quartz. *Chakra:* past life, base, sacral, heart

releasing vows: Turquoise. *Chakra:* past life, brow

rejection: Blue Lace Agate. *Chakra:* past life, heart

resentment: Rhodonite. *Chakra:* past life, base

restraint, emotional or mental: Idocrase. *Chakra:* past life, heart

sexual problems arising from: Malachite (use as polished stone, make remedy by indirect method). *Chakra:* past life, base, sacral

soul agreements, recognition: Wulfenite. *Chakra:* past life, higher crown

tie cutting: Malachite (use as polished stone, make remedy by indirect method), Sunstone, Petalite, Wulfenite, Green Obsidian, Rainbow Obsidian. *Chakra:* past life, base, sacral, solar plexus, brow

thought forms, release Iolite. *Chakra:* past life, brow

wound imprints in etheric body: Sceptre Quartz, Tibetan Black Spot Quartz wand, Charoite, Selenite, Smoky Quartz. *Chakra:* past life

Perception, sense: Sardonyx

Period pains: Serpentine (and see Menstrual problems) *Chakra:* sacral

Perspiration, excessive: Jadeite

  of feet: Gem Silica

Personal power, increase: Carnelian. *Chakra:* base

Personality disorders: Tiger's Eye (wear continuously)

Phobias: Aquamarine, Citrine, Rose Quartz, Chrysocolla, Opal, Blue Tiger's Eye, Rutilated Quartz, Obsidian. *Chakra:* solar plexus, base

Physical:

> **body, discomfort at being in:** Vanadinite (make remedy by indirect method), Phenacite. *Chakra:* earth, base
>
> **endurance, improve:** Sodalite. *Chakra:* earth, base
>
> **exhaustion:** Vanadinite (make remedy by indirect method). *Chakra:* earth, base
>
> **maturation:** Chrysanthemum Stone. *Chakra:* earth, base
>
> **pleasure, share:** Pink Tourmaline. *Chakra:* earth, base
>
> **well-being:** Blue Aventurine. *Chakra:* earth, base

Pigmentation, lack of in hair or skin: Chrysocolla (use crystal remedy as a rinse or massage with stone)

Piles: see Haemorrhoids

Pineal gland: Amethyst, Quartz, Moonstone, Opal, Gem Rhodonite, Sodalite, Ruby, Yellow Labradorite, Petalite. *Chakra:* brow

Pituitary gland: Iolite, Pietersite, Sapphire, Garnet. *Chakra:* brow

Plague, ward off: Ruby (wear continuously), Emerald (take crystal remedy frequently)

Unless otherwise directed, apply crystal over organ or site of symptom, place on appropriate chakra, wear as jewellery, bathe with or take as crystal remedy.

Pleurisy: Pearl

Plutonium pollution: Malachite (use as polished stone, make remedy by indirect method), Smoky Quartz

PMS: Chrysocolla, Opal, Moonstone. *Chakra:* sacral

Pneumonia: Fluorite, Diamond

Pollen allergies: Carnelian

Poison, antidote: Amethyst, Bloodstone, Blue Lace Agate, Diamond, Emerald, Staurolite, Sapphire, Pearl, Zircon. (Tape over stomach, take crystal remedy at frequent intervals.) *Chakra:* solar plexus

Pollutants, anti: Brown Jasper, Malachite (use as polished stone, make remedy by indirect method), Turquoise, Purple Tourmaline. (Place stones in environment to absorb.) *Chakra:* earth

Polarization (re-align to earth's magnetic field): Labradorite

Poltergeists: Chrysocolla

Post-natal depression: Rose Quartz (wear continuously). *Chakra:* solar plexus, sacral

Powerlessness: Tanzanite. *Chakra:* base

Pregnancy: Jasper, Lapis Lazuli, Moonstone, Unakite. *Chakra:* sacral

    support during: Azurite, Peridot, Jasper

    fatigue during: Hematite

Pride: Smoky Quartz. *Chakra:* heart

Unless otherwise directed, apply crystal over organ or site of symptom, place on appropriate chakra, wear as jewellery, bathe with or take as crystal remedy.

Projections, take back: Labradorite, Muscovite, Rhodochrosite. *Chakra:* brow, solar plexus

Prolonged illness: Jade

Prostate, enlarged: Chrysoprase, Obsidian, Zincite

Protection: Labradorite, Malachite (use as polished stone, make remedy by indirect method), Black Tourmaline, Jasper. (Wear continuously.) *Chakra:* throat, higher heart

Protein assimilation: Alexandrite. *Chakra:* solar plexus

Prudishness: Okenite. *Chakra:* base, sacral

Psoriasis: Blue Lace Agate, Labradorite. (Bathe in crystal remedy and apply stone to site.)

Psychic attack: Black Tourmaline, Apache Tear, Rutilated Quartz, Ametrine, Moss Agate, Selenite, Labradorite, Ajoite with Shattuckite. (Wear constantly.) *Chakra:* throat, higher heart

Psychic surgery: Tektite

Psychological shadow: Mahogany Obsidian (do not wear for long periods). *Chakra:* solar plexus

Psychosexual problems: Malachite (use as polished stone, make remedy by indirect method). *Chakra:* base, sacral

Psychosomatic disease: Pink Chalcedony, Iron Pyrite, Kunzite, Amethyst. *Chakra:* brow, higher heart

    stabilize body during changes: Morganite

    understand causes of: Sugilite, Malachite (use as polished stone, make remedy by indirect method)

Unless otherwise directed, apply crystal over organ or site of symptom, place on appropriate chakra, wear as jewellery, bathe with or take as crystal remedy.

Pollutants in atmosphere: Turquoise (wear continuously and purify regularly)

Pulmonary system: Blue Tourmaline

Pulse, irregular: Agate, Charoite. (Wear over heart.)

Pus: Bloodstone

Putrefaction: Pearl

- Q -

Qi, depleted: Kyanite, Magnetite (Lodestone), Zincite.
Chakra: sacral

Quarrels, avoid: Magnetite (Lodestone)

Quinsy: Amber, Topaz. (Wear continuously and/or gargle with crystal remedy.) *Chakra:* throat

---

Unless otherwise directed, apply crystal over organ or site of symptom, place on appropriate chakra, wear as jewellery, bathe with or take as crystal remedy.

- R -

Radiation, counteract: <u>Malachite</u> (use as polished stone, make remedy by indirect method), Jasper, Black Tourmaline, Yellow Kunzite, Smoky Quartz, Sodalite, Quartz. (Place stones around source.) *Chakra:* earth, base

Radioactivity: <u>Malachite</u> (use as polished stone, make remedy by indirect method), <u>Annabergite</u>, Herkimer Diamond. (Place stones around source or wear continuously.)

Radionics: Kunzite

Rashes: Rhyolite

Rebirthing: Carnelian, Red Jasper, Malachite (use as polished stone, make remedy by indirect method) *Chakra:* sacral

Recovery, assist: Ruby in Zoisite

Recuperation: Peridot (wear continuously).

Red blood cells: red stones, Amethyst, Hematite

Reflexology: Larimar (use as tool on reflex points)

Reiki support: Apophyllite (place in room)

Rejection, ease pain of: Rose Quartz. *Chakra:* higher heart

Rejuvenation: Lapis Lazuli, Rhodonite, Sodalite

Relaxation: Amethyst, Aventurine, Fire Agate, Blue

Calcite, Golden Calcite, Dioptase, Fuchsite, Jasper, Peridot, Rhodonite, Magnesite, Smoky Quartz. (Hold or wear, place by bed.) *Chakra:* brow

Release anger and tension: Red Jade. *Chakra:* base

Renal disorders: Jadeite, Nephrite (tape over kidneys)

Renewal: Bloodstone (tape over higher heart chakra)

Repair, assist body to: Blue Quartz

Repetitive strain injury: Fuchsite, Muscovite

Repressed anger: Lapis Lazuli, Rhodonite. *Chakra:* base

Reproductive system: red and orange stones, Moonstone, Carnelian, Rose Quartz, Smoky Quartz, Thulite, Unakite, Tiger's Eye. *Chakra:* base, sacral

> **female:** Wulfenite

> **male:** Variscite

Rescue remedy: Larimar-Rhodochrosite-Rhodonite (take crystal remedy frequently or apply stones.)

Resentment: Peridot. *Chakra:* base

Resistance:

> **to healing:** Morganite, Celestite. *Chakra:* base

> **to change:** Lepidolite. *Chakra:* base, heart

Respiratory system: Candle Quartz, Iron Pyrite, Lapis Lazuli

> **problems:** Apophyllite, Rhodochrosite, Pietersite

Reynauds disease: Aragonite, Hematite

Rheumatism: Agate, Amber, Azurite, Chrysocolla,

Hematite, Carnelian, Chiastolite, Emerald, Labradorite, Malachite (use as polished stone, make remedy by indirect method), Sunstone, Magnetite (Lodestone)

Rickets: Apatite, Calcite (take as crystal remedy), Rutilated Quartz

Ringworm: Calcite, Diamond, Zircon

RNA stabilizing: Ametrine, Azurite with Malachite and Chrysocolla (use as polished stone, make remedy by indirect method)

Unless otherwise directed, apply crystal over organ or site of symptom, place on appropriate chakra, wear as jewellery, bathe with or take as crystal remedy.

- S -

Sacral chakra: orange stones, see Chakras

Sadness: Red Jasper, Sodalite, Ruby. *Chakra:* solar plexus, heart

Saliva, excess: Diamond, Zircon

Scalds: Emerald, Rose Quartz, Rhodonite. (Place stone in cold water and bathe affected part for 20 minutes.)

Scar tissue: Rose Quartz

Schizophrenia: Blue Obsidian, Lepidolite, Ruby, Sugilite, Tiger's Eye, Emerald. *Chakra:* brow, out-of-balance chakras

Sciatica: Kunzite, Lepidolite, Sapphire, Tourmaline, Zircon, Hematite, Rose Quartz

Sciatic nerve: Zircon

Scrofula: Sapphire

Seasonal affective disorder: yellow stones, Sunstone, Topaz. (Wear continuously.) *Chakra:* brow

Security issues: Smithsonite, Idocrase, Chrysoprase. *Chakra:* base

    emotional: Fire Agate, Agate, Yellow Tourmaline. *Chakra:* base, solar plexus

    letting go of: Moldavite. *Chakra:* base

    rebuilding: Smithsonite

Sedation: Magnetite (Lodestone), Rutilated Quartz, Smoky Quartz

Selenium, non-assimilation: Galena (make remedy by indirect method). *Chakra:* solar plexus

Self:

>**acceptance:** Mangano Calcite. *Chakra:* heart, higher heart

>**cleaning stones:** Carnelian, Smoky Quartz, Black Tourmaline. *Chakra:* heart, higher heart

>**esteem:** <u>Rose Quartz</u>, Hemimorphite, Moss Agate, Chrysoberyl, Mangano Calcite, Citrine, Hematite, Fuchsite, Iron Pyrites, Opal, Rhodocrosite, Rhondite, Rhyolite, Sodalite. *Chakra:* base, sacral, heart, higher heart

>**expression:** Kunzite, Blue Lace Agate, Blue Tourmaline, Aqua Aura, Azurite with Chrysocolla. (Wear at throat.) *Chakra:* throat

>**hatred (combating):** Rutilated Quartz. *Chakra:* base

>**healing:** Seraphinite, Larimar, Sunstone, Amber

>**sabotaging behaviour:** Larimar, Tourmalinated Quartz

>**sufficiency:** Jade. *Chakra:* base

>**trust:** Rose Quartz, Kunzite. *Chakra:* sacral

>**worth:** Chrysoberyl, Mangano Calcite, Larimar. *Chakra:* base, sacral

Senile dementia: Chalcedony, Rose Quartz. *Chakra:* brow

Unless otherwise directed, apply crystal over organ or site of symptom, place on appropriate chakra, wear as jewellery, bathe with or take as crystal remedy.

Sense of smell, loss: Idocrase

Sensitivity to light: Selenite

Sensory organs, desensitized: Sardonyx

Septicemia: Quartz

Sexual:

> **abuse, healing:** Rhodochrosite, Pink Agate, Pink Carnelian, Ruby Aura Quartz. *Chakra:* base, sacral
>
> **libido:**
>
>> **loss of:** Fluorite. *Chakra:* base, sacral
>>
>> **imbalances:** Garnet. *Chakra:* base, sacral
>
> **organs:** Jasper, Smoky Quartz, Pink Tourmaline. *Chakra:* base, sacral
>
> **pleasure, prolong:** Jasper. *Chakra:* base, sacral
>
> **tension:** Brown Opal. *Chakra:* base, sacral

Sexually transmitted diseases: Chrysoprase, Malachite (use as polished stone, make remedy by indirect method)

Sexuality: Pyrolusite. *Chakra:* base, sacral

Shame: Rhodochrosite, Sugilite, Larimar. *Chakra:* base

Shingles: Blue Lace Agate, Chrysoprase, Fluorite, Jade, Lapis Lazuli, Chrysoprase, Rose Quartz

Shock: Dioptase, Lapis Lazuli, Obsidian, Rose Quartz, Sugilite. (Take crystal remedy frequently or wear stones constantly.) *Chakra:* solar plexus

Shoulders: Prehnite, Blue Lace Agate, Hawk's Eye, Hiddenite, Larimar, Selenite. *Chakra:* throat

---

Unless otherwise directed, apply crystal over organ or site of symptom, place on appropriate chakra, wear as jewellery, bathe with or take as crystal remedy.

locked: Blue Lace Agate

psychosomatic reasons behind frozen: Hawk's Eye

Shyness: Hematite, Tiger's Eye, Malachite (use as polished stone, make remedy by indirect method). (Wear constantly.)

Sick-building syndrome: Lepidolite, Sodalite, Smoky Quartz. (Place around building, or wear constantly.)

Sighing, excessive: Aquamarine, Morganite, Emerald. *Chakra:* heart

Sight: Aquamarine, Emerald. *Chakra:* brow

Sinus: Azurite, Blue Lace Agate, Black Onyx, Sodalite, Smithsonite, Jet. *Chakra:* brow

Sinusitis: Emerald, Fluorite, Smithsonite, Jet. (Place over nostril or forehead, or inhale crystal essence steam.)

Skeletal system: Septarian, Jade, Snowflake Obsidian, Amazonite, Azurite, Chrysocolla, Calcite, Cuprite, Fluorite, Dendritic Agate, Purple Fluorite, Sardonyx, Iron Pyrite. *Chakra:* brow

    flexibility, improve: Petalite

    strengthen: Fluorite, Blue Lace Agate, Lapis Lazuli, Magnetite (Lodestone)

    support growth in youth: Topaz

Skin: Agate, Amethyst, Aventurine, Azurite, Brown Jasper, Green Jasper, Galena (make remedy by indirect method), Rose Quartz, Sulphur (use as polished crystallized stone, make remedy by indirect method), Topaz

 ageing, reverse: Selenite

 cancer: Emerald

 detoxify: Lepidolite

 disorders: Calcite, Green Aventurine, Rose Quartz, Smithsonite, Agate, Rhodochrosite, Sulphur (use as polished crystallized stone, make remedy by indirect method), Brown and Green Jasper, Zircon, Chrysoprase, Fluorite, Rhyolite, Snowflake Obsidian, Pearl

 growths: Chlorite

 infections: Moss Agate, Sulphur (use as polished crystallized stone, make remedy by indirect method)

Sleep: see Insomnia,

 walking: Moonstone, Topaz. (Wear or place under pillow.)

Sleeping sickness: Amethyst

Sluggishness: red stones, Amethyst, Carnelian, Magnetite (Lodestone), Ruby. *Chakra:* base

Small intestine: Epidote. *Chakra:* sacral

Smell, restore sense of: Red Jasper, Tiger's Eye, Tourmaline

Smoking: Hematite, Peridot. (Wear constantly; dowse for underlying cause and treat accordingly.)

 affecting lungs: Blue Chalcedony

 giving up: Brown Jasper

Snakebite: Emerald, Jasper

Sneezing: Zircon

Spleen chakra: Aventurine, see Chakras

Soft tissue damage: Howlite, Black Onyx

Solar plexus chakra: yellow stones, see Chakras

Sore throat: <u>Blue Lace Agate</u>, Aquamarine, Blue Tourmaline, Blue Jasper, Pyrope Garnet. (Gargle with crystal remedy or wear stone at throat.) *Chakra:* throat

    soothing: Larimar, Pink Opal, Blue Lace Agate. *Chakra:* throat

Sores: Amethyst, Green Aventurine, Chalcedony, Carnelian, Quartz, Ruby, Lapis Lazuli

Sorrow: Sugilite. *Chakra:* heart

Soul: Charoite, Petalite, Azeztulite, Phenacite. (Can be worn constantly.) *Chakra:* higher crown, heart

    dark night of: Black Calcite

    healing: Lavender-violet Smithsonite, Petalite, Ruby in Zoisite, Lavender Jade

    overcome fear in: Charoite

    retrieval: Clear Kunzite, Tangerine Quartz, Selenite, Lavender-violet Smithsonite. *Chakra:* higher heart, brow

Spasms: Amazonite, Aragonite, Azurite, Carnelian, Magnesite, Electric-blue Obsidian, Ruby

Speaking unthinkingly from anger: Chrysoprase. *Chakra:* base, throat

Speech: Blue Agate, Rhodonite. *Chakra:* brow, throat

    defects: Blue Obsidian (must be genuine)

    impediments: Dark Blue Tourmaline, Tourmaline

    therapy, assists: Blue Obsidian (must be genuine)

Spells, protection against: Black Tourmaline, Tiger's Eye.
Chakra: throat, higher heart

Spine: Garnet, Tourmaline, Labradorite, Beryl

    out of alignment: Hiddenite, Labradorite, Magnetite
(Lodestone), Tiger's Eye, Tourmaline

    strengthen base of: Orange Carnelian, Garnet

Spinal:

    column, inflexible: Selenite

    disorders: Garnet

    energy, blocked: Fire Opal, Red Spinel

    injuries: Emerald, Fluorite, Cherry Opal, Selenite

    misalignment: Azurite, Fuchsite, Hematite, Tiger's Eye,
Magnetite (Lodestone), Hiddenite, Labradorite

Spiritual interference: Smoky Quartz, Labradorite,
Amethyst. (Wear constantly). *Chakra:* crown

Spleen: Amber, Aquamarine, Azurite, Bloodstone,
Chalcedony, Citrine, Fluorite, Green Obsidian, Red
Obsidian, Septarian, Chalcedony, Ruby, Peridot, Jade, Yellow
Labradorite, Wulfenite, Zircon, Sunstone. *Chakra:* spleen

    chakra: see Chakras

    deterioration: Yellow and Red Jasper

detoxifying: Bloodstone, Pink Tourmaline

poor functioning, overcome: Honey Calcite, Mookaite

protection: Green Aventurine

stimulating: Ruby, Rubellite (Red Tourmaline)

Spondulytis: Labradorite

Sports injuries: Magnetite (Lodestone) (see also Muscles, page xx)

Stability: Onyx, Black Obsidian (use for short period only), Boji Stones. *Chakra:* base

Stagnant energy: Calcite, Clear Topaz, Smoky Quartz, Quartz. *Chakra:* base

Stamina: Amethyst, Carnelian, Dalmation Jasper, Onyx, Fire Agate, Agate. *Chakra:* base

Stammering: Green Aventurine. *Chakra:* throat, brow

Star children: Moldavite. *Chakra:* higher crown

Steroids, boosting natural: Tiger Iron. *Chakra:* higher heart

Stiff neck: Hawk's Eye, Siberian Blue Quartz. *Chakra:* throat

Stimulating: Tiger's Eye, Carnelian, Jasper. *Chakra:* base

Stitches: Jade

Stomach: Amethyst, Aquamarine, Chrysocolla, Carnelian, Snowflake Obsidian, Amber, Yellow Jasper, Yellow Labradorite, Green Fluorite, Fire Agate, Beryl, Serpentine, Mookaite, Pearl, Jade, Jadeite. *Chakra:* solar plexus

Unless otherwise directed, apply crystal over organ or site of symptom, place on appropriate chakra, wear as jewellery, bathe with or take as crystal remedy.

acidity: Peridot

cramps: Magnesite

pains: Jet, Lapis Lazuli

problems as a result of stress: Chrysoprase

strengthen: Jasper (wear around neck)

swollen: Emerald, Pearl

ulcers: Agate, Pearl, Tiger's Eye, Moonstone, Quartz

upset: Emerald, Bloodstone, Aquamarine, Morganite

Strained muscles: Green Tourmaline (and see Muscles)

Streptococal infections: Fluorite, Amber. (Wear and take crystal remedy frequently.)

Strength, increase: Ruby, Magnetite (Lodestone). *Chakra:* base

Strengthen body: Peridot. *Chakra:* base, earth

Stress: <u>Amethyst</u>, <u>Charoite</u>, <u>Green Aventurine</u>, Beryl, Dioptase, Lapis Lazuli, Magnetite (Lodestone), Herkimer Diamond, Labradorite, Rose Quartz, Rhodonite, Amber, Petalite, Aquamarine, Siberian Quartz, Jasper. *Chakra:* brow, heart, solar plexus

Subconscious blocks: Chrysocolla, Malachite (use as polished stone, make remedy by indirect method)

'Sugary sweet' and inauthentic: Wulfenite. *Chakra:* base

Suicidal tendencies: Smoky Quartz, Amber, Lapis Lazuli. (Wear constantly.)

Unless otherwise directed, apply crystal over organ or site of symptom, place on appropriate chakra, wear as jewellery, bathe with or take as crystal remedy.

Sunburn: Angelite, Siberian Blue Quartz, Larimar, Rose Quartz

Sunstroke: Jadeite, Chrysoprase

Supra-adrenals: Jade

Suppurating wounds: Calcite

Survival instincts, basic: Ruby Aura, Hematite. *Chakra:* base

Sweats: Green Sapphire

Swelling: Amethyst, Anhydrite, Sulphur (use as polished crystallized stone, make remedy by indirect method), Jet, Magnetite (Lodestone)

Swollen:

> **feet:** Jet
>
> **glands and lymphatics:** Jet
>
> **joints:** Malachite (use as polished stone, make remedy by indirect method), Rhodonite (and see Joints)

Synapses: Azurite

- T -

Tachycardia: Garnet (wear over heart)

Taking on other people's feelings: Labradorite, Citrine, Chrysocolla. (Wear constantly.) *Chakra:* solar plexus

Tartar, dissolve: Garnet

Taste, loss of: Staurolite, Stillbite, Topaz, Tourmaline

T-cells: Dioptase, Bloodstone (and see Immune system). *Chakra:* higher heart

Teeth: Calcite, Amethyst, Azurite and Malachite (use as polished stone, make remedy by indirect method), Apatite, Howlite, Aquamarine, Rutilated Quartz, Onyx, Fluorite, Tourmaline, Topaz

    decay: Amazonite

    enamel deficiencies: Idocrase, Onyx

    loose: Jet

    mercury poisoning, antidote: Selenite

    strengthen: Calcite

Teething pain: Amber, Cathedral Quartz

Temperature, regulate: Magnesite, Blue Chalcedony

Temper, out of control: Rose Quartz. *Chakra:* base

Tendonitis: Lepidolite

Tension, release: Carnelian, Rose Quartz, Red Jade,

Muscovite, Herkimer Diamond, Kunzite. *Chakra:* base, heart, solar plexus

Testicles: Amber, Alexandrite, Atacamite, Carnelian, Chrysoprase, Citrine, Gold Calcite, Peach Aventurine, Jadeite, Topaz, Carnelian, Variscite. *Chakra:* base

   diseases of: Zoisite

Third eye (brow chakra): indigo stones, see Chakras, *Chakra:* brow

   activating: Azurite with Malachite (use as polished stone, make remedy by indirect method), Yellow Labradorite, Selenite, Apophyllite, Tibetan Quartz, Lapis Lazuli, Iolite

Throat: <u>Amber</u>, <u>Blue Lace Agate</u>, Apatite, Angelite, Anhydrite, Azurite, Celestite, Blue Jasper, Kyanite, Larimar, Blue Tourmaline, Turquoise, Hematite. *Chakra:* brow

   chakra: blue stones

   infected: Amber (gargle)

   inflammation: Angelite, Aquamarine, Siberian Blue Quartz, Beryl

   relaxed: Amber

   ulcerated: Chrysocolla

Thrombosis: Magnesite

Thrush: Dendritic Chalcedony, Chrysocolla

Thymus (higher heart): Amethyst, Angelite, Aqua Aura,

Blue or Green Tourmaline, Bloodstone, Aventurine, Citrine, Dioptase, Hiddenite, Jadeite, Quartz, Rose Quartz, Septarian. *Chakra:* higher heart

>   **underactive:** Hiddenite, Aqua Aura, Smithsonite, Lapis Lazuli, Peridot

Thyroid: Amber, Aquamarine, Aqua Aura, Azurite, Beryl, Celestite, Blue Tourmaline, Candle Quartz, Citrine, Lapis Lazuli, Idocrase, Kyanite, Sodalite, Turquoise, Rhodonite, Rutilated Quartz, Vanadinite (make remedy by indirect method), Sapphire. *Chakra:* throat

>   **deficiencies:** Blue Lace Agate, Angelite, Harlequin Quartz, Citrine, Kyanite, Lapis Lazuli
>
>   **balance:** Aquamarine
>
>   **regulate:** Lapis Lazuli, Rhodonite
>
>   **stimulate:** Rutilated Quartz, Rhodonite

Tics: Azurite

Tinnitus: Celestite, Hemimorphite

Tiredness: Amethyst, Rose Quartz, Carnelian, Fire Agate, Pyrite. *Chakra:* base

Tissue:

>   **degeneration:** Hematite, Peridot, Carnelian, Citrine, Kunzite, Peridot, Rutilated Quartz, Topaz
>
>   **hardened:** Rhyolite
>
>   **repair:** Angelite, Cherry Opal, Amber, Rutilated Quartz
>
>   **torn:** Rutilated Quartz

Unless otherwise directed, apply crystal over organ or site of symptom, place on appropriate chakra, wear as jewellery, bathe with or take as crystal remedy.

Toes: Aragonite

Toenails: Blue Lace Agate

    fungal infections: Moss Agate

Tonic: Peridot

Tonsillitis: Amber, Blue Lace Agate, Sodalite, Shattuckite, Tourmaline. *Chakra:* base

Tonsils, inflamed: Chrysocolla. *Chakra:* base

Toothache: <u>Amber</u>, Aquamarine, Lapis Lazuli, Malachite (use as polished stone, make remedy by indirect method), Jet

Tourette's syndrome: Celestite

Toxicity: Green Jasper, Sunshine Aura Quartz, Smoky Quartz, Rutilated Quartz, Smoky Quartz. *Chakra:* earth, spleen

Toxins:

    disperse from environment: Chrysanthemum Stone. *Chakra:* base, earth, spleen, solar plexus

    ingested: Iron Pyrite (take crystal remedy frequently). *Chakra:* base, earth, spleen, solar plexus

    remove: Ametrine, Yellow Apatite, Celestite, Moss Agate, Serpentine, Iolite. *Chakra:* base, earth, spleen, solar plexus

    strengthen resistance to: Beryl. *Chakra:* base, earth, spleen, solar plexus

Tranquillizer: Amethyst

Tranquillity: pink and green stones, Jade, Emerald.

Unless otherwise directed, apply crystal over organ or site of symptom, place on appropriate chakra, wear as jewellery, bathe with or take as crystal remedy.

Chakra: higher heart

Transformation: Charoite. *Chakra:* higher heart

Trauma: Mangano Calcite, Fuchsite, Moss Agate, Rose Quartz, Malachite (use as polished stone, make remedy by indirect method), Lavender Jade. (Take remedy frequently, hold stone.) *Chakra:* solar plexus

Trapped nerve: Kunzite

Travel sickness: Jasper, Malachite (use as polished stone, make remedy by indirect method)

Triple burner meridian, rebalance: Fire Agate, Fire Opal

Truth, speak: Chrysocolla. *Chakra:* throat

Tuberculosis: Amber, Dioptase, Emerald, Morganite, Topaz, Blue Sapphire, Pearl

Tumours: Amethyst, Rose Quartz, Fluorite, Petalite, Bloodstone, Malachite (use as polished stone, make remedy by indirect method), Jet, Sardonyx, Sapphire

- U -

Ulcers: Ametrine, Calcite, Chrysocolla, Fluorite, Peridot, Siberian Quartz, Rhodonite, Green Aventurine, Tiger's Eye, Sapphire, Moonstone, Tourmaline

    eyes: Sapphire

    gastric: Agate

    intestinal: Ametrine

    mouth: Ruby

    skin: Blue Lace Agate, Calcite, Ruby, Emerald

    stomach: Blue Lace Agate, Emerald, Siberian Blue Quartz, Peridot, Rhodonite, Sapphire, Sunstone

    throat: Chrysocolla

    varicose: Bloodstone, Blue Lace Agate, Ruby

Unacceptable thoughts and feelings: Picture Jasper. *Chakra:* solar plexus, brow

Unconditional love: Kunzite, Magnesite, Rose Quartz, Rhodochrosite. (Wear continuously or place over higher heart.) *Chakra:* higher heart

Ungroundedness: Boji Stones, Hematite, Smoky Quartz. *Chakra:* earth, base

Upset stomach with headache: Ametrine

Uro-genital tract: Kyanite, Blue Aventurine. *Chakra:* sacral

Unless otherwise directed, apply crystal over organ or site of symptom, place on appropriate chakra, wear as jewellery, bathe with or take as crystal remedy.

Urinary ailments: Blue Lace Agate, Amber, Jadeite, Jasper, Red Calcite, Ruby, Jade

Urinary system: Citrine, Jade

Urinary tract infections: Yellow or Green Zincite (according to colour of urine)

Uterus: Wulfenite, Agate. *Chakra:* sacral

Uterine bleeding: Jasper. *Chakra:* sacral

- V -

Vagina: Carnelian. *Chakra:* sacral

Vampirism of heart energy: Aventurine, Ruby. *Chakra:* solar plexus, heart, higher heart

Vascular cramps: Magnesite

Veins: Variscite, Pyrolusite, Snowflake Obsidian, Galena (make remedy by indirect method), Ruby, Rhodochrosite, Rhyolite, Golden Healer, Smithsonite

    elasticity: Smithsonite, Variscite

    strengthen walls: Rutilated Quartz, Sapphire

    varicose: Topaz, Tourmaline, Blue John, Aquamarine, Amber, Blue Lace Agate, Opal, Rhodonite

Venereal disease: Zircon. *Chakra:* base

Venomous bites: Emerald

Vertebrae: Labradorite

Vertigo: Morganite, Lapis Lazuli, Malachite (use as polished stone, make remedy by indirect method), Rose Quartz, Red Jasper, Blue Sapphire

Vibrational change, facilitate: Ajoite, Blue Lace Agate, Charoite, Danburite, Celestite, Cathedral Quartz, Selenite, Kunzite, Shattuckite, Tanzanite, Phenacite, Moldavite, Violet-Lavender Amethyst, Violet Muscovite, Blue Boji

---

Unless otherwise directed, apply crystal over organ or site of symptom, place on appropriate chakra, wear as jewellery, bathe with or take as crystal remedy.

Stones, Seraphinite. (Wear stones frequently or keep within reach and hold frequently.) *Chakra:* higher heart, higher crown

Vigour, improve: Peridot. *Chakra:* base

Violence, negate: Apatite, Bloodstone, Rose Quartz. (Keep in environment.) *Chakra:* base

Viral infections: Fluorite, Turquoise. *Chakra:* higher heart

Virility, increase: red or orange stones, Red-black Obsidian, Lapis Lazuli, Ruby in Zoisite. *Chakra:* base, sacral

Viruses, anti: Fluorite. *Chakra:* higher heart

Vision:

> **poor:** Emerald, Clear Fluorite, Topaz, Ulexite. *Chakra:* brow

> **obscured:** Clear Fluorite, Ulexite. *Chakra:* brow

Vitality, increase: Amber, Black Tourmaline, Red-black Obsidian, Fire Opal, Jade, Rutilated Quartz, Ruby, Red Jasper, Carnelian. *Chakra:* base

Vitality, overcome lack of: red stones, Agate, Aventurine, Bloodstone, Chalcedony, Cerussite, Dioptase, Emerald, Ruby, Zircon, Rhodochrosite, Red Calcite. *Chakra:* base

Vitamin, non-absorption: Carnelian, Garnet. *Chakra:* solar plexus

> **A and E:** Blue-green Selenite
> **B:** Tiger Iron, Rhyolite
> **C and D:** Apache Tear

Unless otherwise directed, apply crystal over organ or site of symptom, place on appropriate chakra, wear as jewellery, bathe with or take as crystal remedy.

Vocal cords: Amber, Blue Lace Agate, Blue Calcite, Rhodonite, Sodalite, Tourmaline. (Wear or take crystal remedy.) *Chakra:* throat

Voice, weak: Blue Kyanite. *Chakra:* throat

Vomiting: Emerald, Lapis Lazuli, Moonstone. *Chakra:* solar plexus

- W -

Walking difficulties: Albite, Brown Aragonite

Warts: Calcite, Emerald, Apatite and sea salt

Wasting diseases: Carnelian, Red Jasper, Magnetite (Lodestone)

Water purifier: Lithium Quartz (leave for 20 minutes)

Water retention: Mookaite, Anhydrite, Moonstone

Water–salt imbalances: Jade

Weak:

> **energy field:** Quartz (hold in front of solar plexus)
>
> **muscles:** Amethyst, Hematite

Weakness, general: Amethyst, Hematite, Turquoise

Weather sensitivity: Moss Agate, Blue Chalcedony.
Chakra: brow

Well-being, promote: Dioptase, Green Aventurine.
Chakra: higher heart

Weight:

> **control:** Angelite, Apatite
>
> **loss:** Unakite, Seraphinite, Green Tourmaline, Prehnite
>
> **over:** Kyanite, Seraphinite, Green Tourmaline
>
> **under:** Danburite

Whitlow: Fluorite, Topaz, Tourmaline

Unless otherwise directed, apply crystal over organ or site of symptom, place on appropriate chakra, wear as jewellery, bathe with or take as crystal remedy.

Whooping cough: Amber, Blue Lace Agate, Topaz

Will-power: Rose Quartz, Black Onyx, Tiger's Eye, Ruby, Garnet. *Chakra:* base

Will to be cured: Garnet

Will to live, increase: Opal

Wisdom: Amethyst, Carnelian. *Chakra:* crown

Worry: Red Jasper

Workaholic: Staurolite, Tanzanite

Wounds: Amber, Fluorite, Mookaite, Rhodonite, Sapphire, Rose Quartz, Ruby, Garnet

Wrinkles, remove: Fluorite, Ulexite. (Bathe skin in crystal remedy.)

Unless otherwise directed, apply crystal over organ or site of symptom, place on appropriate chakra, wear as jewellery, bathe with or take as crystal remedy.

- X -

X-rays, prevent damage from: Amazonite, Herkimer Diamond, Malachite (use as polished stone, make remedy by indirect method), Lepidolite, Smoky Quartz. (Wear constantly, rub crystal remedy over site, take crystal remedy frequently.)

- Y -

Yin–yang imbalances: Kyanite, Celestite, Merlinite, Onyx, Hematite with Rutile. *Chakra:* base

- Z -

Zinc absorption: Galena (make remedy by indirect method). *Chakra:* solar plexus

---

Unless otherwise directed, apply crystal over organ or site of symptom, place on appropriate chakra, wear as jewellery, bathe with or take as crystal remedy.

SUPPLIERS

Crystal Clear: David Eastoe: www.petaltone.co.uk
Crystals: www.exquisitecrystals.com,
www.earthworksuk.com,

FURTHER READING by Judy Hall

The Crystal Bible: volumes 1-3 (Godsfield Press, London,
Walking Stick Press, U.S.A.)

Crystal Prescriptions volumes 1-6
(O-Books, Arlesford, 2005-2017)

The Crystal Wisdom Healing Oracle (Watkins Books,
London 2016)

*101 Power Crystals: the ultimate guide to magical crystals,
gems, and stones for healing and transformation*
(Fair Winds, USA, Quarto, London)

*Earth Blessings: using crystals for personal energy clear,
earth healing and environmental enhancement*
(Watkins Books, London 2014)

*Crystals and Sacred Sites: Using crystals to harness the
power of sacred landscapes* (Fair Winds, USA 2012)

*The Crystal Experience: your complete crystal workshop in a
book* (Godsfield, London 2012)

The Crystal Encyclopedia (Godsfield Press, Fair Winds
USA revised edition 2013)

Psychic Self Protection: Using crystals to change your life
(Hay House)

*Good Vibrations: energy enhancement, psychic protection and
space clearing* (Flying Horse Publications, Bournemouth)

Book of Psychic Development (Flying Horse Publications,
Bournemouth)

The Holy Spirit's Interpretation of the New Testament
A course in Understanding and Acceptance
Regina Dawn Akers
Following on from the strength of *A Course In Miracles*,
NTI teaches us how to experience the love and oneness
of God.
Paperback: 978-1-84694-085-9 ebook: 978-1-78099-083-5

The Message of A Course In Miracles
A translation of the text in plain language
Elizabeth A. Cronkhite
A translation of *A Course In Miracles* into plain, everyday
language for anyone seeking inner peace. The
companion volume, *Practicing a Course In Miracles*, offers
practical lessons and mentoring.
Paperback: 978-1-84694-319-5 ebook: 978-1-84694-642-4

Thinker's Guide to God
Peter Vardy
An introduction to key issues in the philosophy of
religion.
Paperback: 978-1-90381-622-6

Your Simple Path
Find happiness in every step
Ian Tucker
A guide to helping us reconnect with what is really
important in our lives.
Paperback: 978-1-78279-349-6 ebook: 978-1-78279-348-9

365 Days of Wisdom
Daily Messages To Inspire You Through The Year
Dadi Janki
Daily messages which cool the mind, warm the heart
and guide you along your journey.
Paperback: 978-1-84694-863-3 ebook: 978-1-84694-864-0

Body of Wisdom
Women's Spiritual Power and How it Serves
Hilary Hart
Bringing together the dreams and experiences of women
across the world with today's most visionary spiritual
teachers.
Paperback: 978-1-78099-696-7 ebook: 978-1-78099-695-0

The Ecology of the Soul
A Manual of Peace, Power and Personal Growth for Real
People in the Real World
Aidan Walker
Balance your own inner Ecology of the Soul to regain
your natural state of peace, power and wellbeing.
Paperback: 978-1-78279-850-7 ebook: 978-1-78279-849-1

Not I, Not other than I
The Life and Teachings of Russel Williams
Steve Taylor, Russel Williams
The miraculous life and inspiring teachings of one of the
World's greatest living Sages.
Paperback: 978-1-78279-729-6 ebook: 978-1-78279-728-9

On the Other Side of Love
A Woman's Unconventional Journey Towards Wisdom
Muriel Maufroy
When life has lost all meaning, what do you do?
Paperback: 978-1-78535-281-2 ebook: 978-1-78535-282-9

Practicing A Course In Miracles
A Translation of the Workbook in Plain Language and
With Mentoring Notes
Elizabeth A. Cronkhite
The practical second and third volumes of The Plain-
Language *A Course in Miracles*.
Paperback: 978-1-84694-403-1 ebook: 978-1-78099-072-9

Quantum Bliss
The Quantum Mechanics of Happiness, Abundance, and
Health
George S. Mentz
Quantum Bliss is the breakthrough summary of success
and spirituality secrets that customers have been
waiting for.
Paperback: 978-1-78535-203-4 ebook: 978-1-78535-204-1

The Upside Down Mountain
Mags MacKean
A must-read for anyone weary of chasing success and
happiness – one woman's inspirational journey
swapping the uphill slog for the downhill slope.
Paperback: 978-1-78535-171-6 ebook: 978-1-78535-172-3

Your Personal Tuning Fork
The Endocrine System
Deborah Bates
Discover your body's health secret, the endocrine
system, and 'twang' your way to sustainable health!
Paperback: 978-1-84694-503-8 ebook: 978-1-78099-697-4

Readers of ebooks can buy or view any of these bestsellers
by clicking on the live link in the title. Most titles are
published in paperback and as an ebook. Paperbacks are
available in traditional bookshops. Both print and
ebook formats are available online.

Find more titles and sign up to our readers' newsletter at
http://www.johnhuntpublishing.com/mind-body-spirit

Follow us on Facebook at https://www.facebook.com/OBooks/
and Twitter at https://twitter.com/obook